Beddy Von,

Thank-you for your support! I wish you the BEST Birthday you have ever had!

"Never Give up"

Keep Shining bright! May the Lord continue to bless you! —♥ Tabatha Wilson

GUILT, HURT, SHAME,

But Not Defeat

BY TABATHA WILSON

Guilt, Hurt, Shame, But Not Defeat
By Tabatha Wilson

Softcover ISBN 978-1-64338-330-9

Reformation Publishers, Inc.
14 S. Queen Street, Mt. Sterling, Kentucky 40353, USA
www.reformationpublishers.com
Email rpublisher@aol.com
Orders 1-800-765-2464
Information 859-520-3757
Text 606-359-2064
Fax 859-520-3357
Printed and bound in the United States of America

CONTENTS

Guilt, Hurt, Shame, But Not Defeat

CHAPTER 1

The Beginning of Life

Do you carry the guilt of your past, the hurt that others caused, or shame from what you have done? Did you just bury the secrets deep down and assume they would someday go away? Or did you choose just to live with it? Yet later in life, you realized that you have never healed? I did, too! I knew that for me to be all that God wanted me to be, I was going to have to surrender to him. I asked myself, "What is normal? What does normal look like?" I never understood a real normal. Until suddenly, my perspective was refined.

Human nature makes us so quick to judge others before we really know who they are. The truth is that it's a form of bullying, done silently. Those who bully are really only covering up pain they have buried. In order for them to feel good about themselves, they have to prey on someone else. It gives them a sense of gratification, a feeling of power over their weaknesses. Sadly, everyone has a secret, in one aspect or the other, and those secrets are bondage that you may not realize exists.

Have you been guilty in taking pride in sinning? Not sure? Let me explain: When living in sin, we sometimes do it unknowingly. It can be done through enjoyment of gossiping about that "druggie" that needs to get their life together, watching pornography, getting hyped watching someone fighting out of anger, lying, thieving, or manipulating. These are just a few of many things that are toxic to the pain of others. Have you ever thought about why they do what they do? A majority of these types of people, including yourself, has direct issues related to a situation in their past. Sexual assault, rape, trafficking, exploitation, bullying, poverty, or hate can impact a person's mental state and cause confusion as to who they really are. These issues are traumatic, painful, and agonizing and leave their prey feeling worthless. As a result, many turn to the very thing that will numb that pain and give them a false value in life. Their hope is nonexistent and their strength is feeble. If you are or ever have been a victim, it's not your fault! And, you are NOT defined by the things you have done or been through! Christ PAID the ultimate sacrifice for your freedom!

My story begins here...

My parents married at a young age. My mom, Valerie, was 16 years old and my dad, Mike, was 24 years old. Despite their age gap, they met through family members on my mom's side and quickly fell in love. Both of them were high school dropouts and didn't have the desire to pursue a higher education. In their day, that was something seemingly normal, especially in the small town where we lived. Much like today, many people lived in poverty and could not afford a college education. Others did not even know where to begin.

My mom came from a sheltered, split home with several siblings, whereas my father came from a home with both parents. However, his home wasn't picture perfect, and they had their own struggles. Mental health and anger issues were genetic from my papaw's side, and he put my mamaw through a lot of trauma. My dad seemed to be the only one of his two siblings who was cursed with the issues of his father. He always claimed that he was OK, and on the outside you would agree. However, on the inside, he battled many untold secrets.

Shortly after taking their vows, my mom found out she was pregnant with me. My mom had a lot to learn about being an adult because she was so young. Before turning 17, she gave birth to me, and motherhood became natural for her.

Upon my arrival, my parents moved from Clay City, Kentucky, into a small apartment in Lexington, Kentucky. My dad began working for a local Domino's Pizza to make a small income to get by. And my mom was a stay-at-home mother, caring for me. Money was always a struggle, and living in Lexington ended after two short years.

We ended up moving back to our hometown, located in the mountains of eastern Kentucky. Powell County had a population of approximately 11,000 people in the early 1990s. There wasn't much the small town offered other than the historic beauty it held. However, my parents knew their family was there and their support could make it a bit easier for them. This necessary move had to happen due to the unknown circumstances they faced.

Following two years of marriage, my dad began staying out all night and not returning home until the late morning. Mom always questioned his whereabouts but continued to push forward for my well-being. Honestly, I believe Mom felt less self-confident and trapped due to the age difference and lack of self-income. Similarly, I remember my mom saying she never ate a real cheeseburger until after she married my dad. This statement alone tells me that she did not get out much and did not have many life experiences. Therefore, she was not developed for the battles life was to bring.

We settled in a small apartment located in the center of town. My mom received a big surprise, realizing she was pregnant once again. She was 19 years old and taking on another huge responsibility for which only God could prepare her. Both of my parents were so excited, and so was I. At the time, I was at only three years old. I loved baby dolls, and I was ready to care for my bubby. After nine long months, my mom gave birth to my baby brother. He was given a powerful name from the Bible— Joseph! In the Bible, Joseph was favored, and God used him in a mighty way. In some sense, my brother was the same.

Upon his arrival and coming home, the bond that grew between us was unbreakable. I was immediately attached to my little brother. My mom let me help her feed him and do some of the nonstop duties. However, when it came to changing a poopy diaper, I didn't want any part of it. No way!! He was such a good baby and rarely cried. He truly made our family complete in every way! Our family was so happy because of him. I couldn't ever imagine it being any different, but God decided he had other plans for his life.

One cold, rainy morning, we woke up to a nightmare that changed all of our lives forever. My baby brother lay in his bassinet, lifeless. Blood-tinged froth was flowing from his nose, mouth, and ears. That day, he became a victim to Sudden Infant Death Syndrome. I clearly remember screaming and crying in anguish. My parents were grief-stricken and broken. There was no calm, no peace, and it seemed nothing could take that pain away.

Paramedics quickly arrived on scene and escorted me to my room to console me. I specifically remember a couple of them trying to occupy me by turning on my basic Nintendo and playing Mario with me. My eyes were so full of tears that I couldn't see the small TV screen in front of me. I kept asking questions and was left with no answers. Not knowing what was happening and why, I had no choice but to wait in my room until the scene was clear. Can you imagine what was happening in my young mind? The visions of what I had seen replayed over and over. Yeah, it was the start of a traumatic life for me, and little did I know, it wouldn't stop there.

I waited for what seemed hours before the scene was clear, and I was taken to my granny Virgie's house. It may not have actually taken that long, but it felt like forever. I watched her wait by the corded phone that hung on the wall, pacing the floors and offering to fix me anything I wanted. I remember the loud ring of that phone, and the expression on her face said it all. She wept and quietly asked questions. Shortly before the call, she told me, "Don't cry baby. Your bubby is going to be OK!" She wasn't there though, and she didn't see what I had seen. I found no peace in her encouragement, and I just wanted to be with my parents. I knew that something was wrong, and I was so scared.

My parents came to Granny's house and began preparation for the next dreadful steps to lay his little body to rest. It was very emotional, but they tried their best to keep it together for me. However, I was feeding off of their emotion, and I felt the same sadness. My young mind went through a lot of misunderstanding and chaos. I had never felt this before, and I did not know how to release it. I just didn't understand!!! How do babies die? I only thought old people did. This was the day that I learned death has no limits, and it can take anyone.

The grim day came, and we went to the services being held for Joseph. The atmosphere was smothering, traumatic, and extremely sad. My mother lay across the casket, and she grieved uncontrollably. You could hear her cries from a distance as they rang out in a echo. I was brought to the front to say my goodbyes. My parents held me as I leaned over to kiss his cold, firm forehead. I could feel the difference in touch of his face on my lips, which was my first encounter with feeling death in its form. My heart ached. A knot was in my throat, and tears streamed steadily.

The funeral home scent was a fragrance I would never forget. The smell of fresh roses still sends chills up my spine. That odor lingered under my nose for years to come and would trigger me. Due to this, I am certain I had undiagnosed PTSD. I adopted anger, anxiety, and confusion at an abnormally young age. I had to learn the hard way about the feeling of loving someone and having that person being taken away. I feared death, and I was so afraid my parents would be next. I remember, as I got older, I had vivid nightmares of car accidents and people dying. This was very common for me, and I was tormented by the hurt.

Days turned into months, and months into years. They say, "Time brings healing." For us, that didn't happen. We didn't mention Joseph or talk about our feelings much. Mom was deeply depressed and couldn't talk about it. My dad and mom dealt with this deep-rooted burden, and it haunted them every day. There was no normalcy after this, and it was like my family disconnected. To any mother who has lost a child, I pray for you. I saw my mother deal with this for many years, and still to this day it hurts her. I speak peace into your life, and pray you find comfort in knowing your child is in the arms of God.

With all of my many fears, I was afraid to sleep alone. I hated when the darkness of night fell, and I grew very dependent on my parents for everything. I was scared of my own shadow! I recall having illusions of scary shadows or blood-stained walls that intruded my mind. I always thought something was out to get me! At night time, if I needed to go to the bathroom, to keep from putting my feet on the floor, I would literally pee on myself or hold it until morning. My mind and body were crippled in fear, and I had no control over it.

I was four, almost five, when I began kindergarten. We had moved from the apartment to a small brown trailer in the "bottoms." The bottoms was an area that had a lot of low-income housing and apartments. Drugs and crime became known in this area, later in time. We now lived closer to my granny and aunt whom I adored. I was constantly at one of their homes, cooking, watching my favorite shows, or just being a kid in some way. Throughout spending time at their house, I realized how different our lifestyle was from theirs. I longed for the stability they could give me, and I grew attached to them.

When I was little, I was a chubby girl with blonde locks, like Shirley Temple. I had a heart of gold, an old soul, and a sassy attitude that brought silence to any room. I didn't have a care in the world and very little home training. I was different from other kids and stuck out like a sore thumb. There was a lot for me to learn, especially starting kindergarten. I didn't listen to a word anyone would tell me, and I had a hard time being told no.

Beginning my journey as a kindergartener, I did have a lot of disadvantages and lessons that I had to learn. Starting school was kind of a big deal for me. Being the child I was, I had to learn to get out of the "it's my way or the highway" mind-set. My teacher, Mrs. Kirkland, was surely an angel sent to teach me. I started out coloring everything in sight purple. I never used any of the other 23 crayons in the box, only purple. When I began writing, my letters were so large! I used more lined alphabet papers than the other kids and had a hard time staying between the lines. I was the loudest student in class and picked up bad habits at a young age. I even stole a girl's bag of Doritos in class and ate them! I'll take the time now to apologize for that. Mrs. Kirkland always remained patient and collected with me although I'm sure there was a time or two she wanted to whoop my behind.

As I began making new friends and my character developed, I realized my struggles were different from others. I was not like them. I was unique, and did things that made no sense sometimes. At first, it was challenging for me to make new friends. However, that all changed when my daddy started showing up at all my school functions with Domino's pizza. He would deliver it to our classroom and brighten the room with his personality. The kids would say, "You're so lucky"! "I wish my family owned Domino's Pizza!" I just went with it because I felt like somebody. I lived a lie and would have never admitted it.

Not only did the kids love my dad but the ladies did as well. His dark hair and icy baby blue eyes made him a catch. He was a little stocky built and kept a thin, prickly shadow beard. What was so attractive about that? I don't know. His personality got him by because he knew he was the man! A lot of people close to us called him, "K-Y sexy man," short for "Kentucky's sexy man." If that tells you anything (sarcasm)! He was somewhat of a big deal to students and teachers in my school. Not just in school, but everywhere else, too. He was highly thought of and respected.

Over time, I picked up on some of dad's personality traits and imitated them myself. It worked for him, so why not for me? Some kids began calling me, "Rich kid." Truth be told, I loved it because I was anything but rich. My dad was a people pleaser, and I was, too. I was taught, "Even if you don't have something, act like you do." My dad was always competing with my uncle who was favored in life. He couldn't stand to hear about his new cars, vacations, or success. He hated it! Yeah, he was jealous of him for a long time but would have never admitted it! If you're reading this and have jealousy toward someone, I pray that stronghold off your life! You are SOMEBODY, too, and don't think any different about yourself.

My parents both worked day and night at the pizza joint. After school and on weekends, I stayed at my granny's house. Granny was my inspiration in life! She helped me with my homework, taught me how to cook, and gave the best back rubs!! Oh, there is nothing like the love of a grandmother. Now my papaw was rather crazy. He was a former army vet and had a diagnosis of schizophrenia. He talked to himself and rubbed his hands raw all day. I was used to his disease, but there were times it got a little scary. When he would forget to take his meds, he went on a rampage. I was good at adding gas to the fire by picking at him and making him angry.

I found enjoyment in pulling the long hairs on Papaw's arms and then running! He would get up and chase me like a maniac, threatening to beat the devil out of me. When the time came to confess to Granny, I always blamed him. With me being the only grandbaby, and my dad being the first born of her three kids, I got away with everything. I took advantage and manipulated any situation I could. Looking back, I was the girl version of "Dennis the Menace"! I was good at doing the things I wasn't supposed to.

With my parents, I couldn't use all of my manipulation tactics. They would catch on to it quicker than Mamaw. However, due to their exhaustion from their busy schedules, there was a lot that went unnoticed. They would compete with each other all the time, and frustrations stayed high. Dad said a lot of hurtful things that would bring Mom down all the time. She was mentally drained from his badgering, and belittling. Mom was a strong woman to take some of the things my dad said to her.

Dear husband or wife, if you constantly say hurtful things to your spouse out of anger, please seek help. No one deserves to be talked down to or made to feel less than others. If you have children, they are watching and listening to every word. While they are young, they may not understand it, but I promise when they get older it sticks with them. Listen to me, I sought love in all of the wrong places because I didn't know how a man was supposed to treat a woman. I didn't know what love really looked like, and it messed me up!! Love each other as if it's your last time to love. Tomorrow isn't promised, and neither is the rest of today. When you feel anger rise up, speak over yourself and claim victory!! The enemy is out to kill, steal, and destroy your marriage, and home!! Joshua 24:15 reads, "And if it seem evil unto you to serve the Lord, choose you this day whom ye will serve; whether the gods which your fathers served that were on the other side of the flood, or the gods of the Amorites, in whose land ye dwell: but as for me and my house, we will serve the Lord. Amen!"

Moving on, Mom was always a naturally pretty lady. She kept her dark brown hair short. She was thick in the waist and had the prettiest green eyes ever! They stuck out like the contacts you see people getting to create their dream look. She was modest in her way and very natural. Her self-esteem was nothing like my dad's. However, her temper was a force to be reckoned with. Close friends of theirs made the joke that she "wore the pants in the house." That was not always the truth, but secretly she tried to keep control.

People say that opposites attract, but in their case I believe that was an urban legend. Yet they made it work, and Mom didn't give up. People who didn't know them probably thought they were perfect together. They seemed to maintain that image well. There were good times, but the bad outweighed the good. Mom always said, "I don't believe in divorce!" Sticking to her belief, they continued their toxic marriage and never had help. I respect her for keeping that covenant and pushing through. However, there were times that I wanted to see her free from it because her pain affected me, too.

CHAPTER 2
Dale Drive

My first-grade year was approaching and my parents decided they wanted to move 20 minutes away to a larger town that had a Domino's. I was surprised they were actually going to move away from Granny, being that we lived close to her all their life. I became excited and nervous about attending a new school and building new friendships. I still looked forward to the new opportunity though and didn't think twice about the rest. I was sailing out on a new adventure.

The moving truck was packed and we were officially hitting the highway. Mom, Dad, and I pulled up to a beautiful three-story, Victorian-style home located in town. My eyes lit up seeing my huge bedroom. Although I enjoyed sleeping with my parents, the large room was irresistible. Compared to my previous room, it was a mini house in itself. As we settled in, my dad immediately went back to work. Mom explained how living here would allow them more freedom and they would rotate their schedule so that one of them would always be with me. That made me even happier to get to spend more quality time with the both of them.

Upon starting school, I adapted to my new environment. Every weekend, my mom would take me out for dinner and a movie or to Kids' Place. She kept me entertained, and I always had fun. At that point, I had the life any kid would enjoy. With Mom being home more than Dad, we became closer than ever before. I loved having more time with her and making memories. Likewise, I always looked forward to our weekends together.

Shortly after moving in this large home, I woke up one morning covered in the stings of fire ants. The house had previous issues that my parents were unaware of. This unfortunate situation led us to moving immediately without hesitation. My parents found another house located on Dale Drive just down the street from the previous one. This was a really nice home that was definitely a level above how we were used to living. I was glad that the ants attacked me because we were blessed with something even better.

I became friends with the neighbor's daughter across the street. Her name was Emerald. Emerald was a popular girl, and it was obvious her family inherited wealth. Her mom was snooty and seemed to have a lot of secrets. She was always gone and rarely cared for Emerald. At the time, I didn't understand that this was not normal. Emerald was maybe a year older than I and left to care for herself. It was as if she had no rules! Most of the time we played outside and didn't ever go in her house. However, one day she snuck me in while her mom was gone.

Upon taking me into the house, she said, "I have something to show you. You can never tell anyone else." I nodded in agreement. She opened the door to a closet where two older girls sat scrunched together. They didn't have nice clothes on like Emerald had. They looked dirty in appearance, frail, and scared. Their arms were bent up, holding their hands near their face. I remember her saying something mean to them and slamming the door.

I asked, "Who are they?"

She replied, "Our maids!" I never questioned the odd circumstances of why they were in that closet. After that day, I never saw them again and never lost the image of them being hidden in that closet. If only I was wise enough to have helped them! If there was ever a day that I would like to relive, it would have been that one.

A short time later, Mom and Dad couldn't afford to pay the bills, forcing us to move back to our hometown again. We moved into an apartment that, once again, was located in the Bottoms. They said they needed to save money. This was the beginning of life unraveling and instability taking place. My childhood was like a rollercoaster of ups and downs, and I just went through the motions of moving from place to place and facing the unknowns of what adventure would come next. As a kid, I didn't know this wasn't normal. I mean, what was normal?

My dad was staying gone again and took on the habit of drinking. It caused nothing but aggressive behavior and a toxic environment. Mom received a phone call from my granny, and she quickly realized she was losing grip on my dad. Granny told her that my dad called and said he'd signed himself into Charter Ridge. Mom was unaware of how bad his problems were up until this moment. He didn't call her with his one phone call; instead he called his mom. My mom seemed to panic and took me with her to the mental hospital where he was staying. During our visit, he exposed the dark truth. He had been stealing thousands of dollars from my uncle's business and claimed he was hearing voices! The Ridge transferred him to an institution located in Harrodsburg, Kentucky, where he received long-term care.

Dad would call Mom and check in on us. After getting out, it wasn't long before they split apart due to toxic indifferences. My mom stayed with her brother and his wife. I refused to leave Dad because I wanted to take care of him. At this time, I favored him more and knew I could get out more. Dad always kept me entertained! We would go to local wrestling shows, golfing, and do a lot of fishing. The crazy part was that I liked them better apart than together. However, my mom was not going to stay away from me for long and decided to come back.

Soon enough my parents mended their little "pow wow," and got back together. From there we moved into a blue trailer beside my granny's house. My dad never went back to work and applied for disability due to his

sickness. He was diagnosed with heart disease and diabetes. We fell right back into the old routine. Mom had
no choice but to work day and night at this point to keep
us fed. Nothing changed now that my parents got back
together. They continued arguing and fighting all the
time. My dad continued living a double life and would
still stay gone, doing God knows what. So I stayed at
Granny's all the time.

My home became very unstable and Mom just went
off the edge. She would not only question Dad about other women but demanded him to tell her what secrets he
had. She noticed a lot of money was being spent, money
she knew they didn't have. She couldn't figure out where
it was coming from. He was bringing home gifts to me
every night and household items at random. She knew
something was seriously wrong, but he swore that it was
his money. When asked, Dad would tell her, "Shut up
and don't worry about it!" Mom had no power over it
and chose to live with it. In seeing these arguments and
behaviors, I adopted his toxic personality traits. People
please protect your children. They see, they hear, and
they do!

CHAPTER 3
Exposed

*F*ollowing the theft issue with my dad, my mom was the type of person who always wanted to do the right thing. She wanted Dad to make it right but that wasn't happening. His pride was too high, and he would rather say nothing at all. His reputation was ruined, and I think he felt my uncle always owed him something. He didn't wear jealousy well at all and was not ready for deliverance. He drank and gambled to numb his embarrassment. He started seeing a psychiatrist and received treatment for his mental illness. He claimed he heard voices and saw my dead brother all the time. He was comfortable with openly discussing these things but even more comfortable with holding on to them.

Dad seemed healthier at times and would say that it was just a crazy spell he went through. He declared that he was changed and wanted to give us a better life. He started working at a gas station in town, under the table, and began going to church while he awaited disability.

After a short time, he said the Lord called him to be a preacher. So he started evangelizing and was attending small holiness churches close by. He would play bass guitar during the worship part of the service and preach afterward from time to time. Everything was good for a while, but he slowly fell off the wagon again. No one in the church knew about the issues he had and seemed to believe in him. If you are this preacher, or musician, the enemy has no authority over your life! Please allow God to heal you, and set you free! Believe it, speak it, and receive it! Amen! The enemy wants to devour the people of God, and it is time to take back all that he has stolen from you.

From one extreme to the next, he gambled all the time at the gas station. There was a rumor going around that he was stealing money again. He lost his job, and Mom became furious. His health started declining even more afterward. He had a massive heart attack and was diagnosed as a type 1 diabetic. Mom took on another heavy load and worked for a food court in town to pay bills. Dad became completely disabled and incapable of working. He continued trying for disability benefits and was told it could take years to get it. He went from doctor to doctor trying to speed up the process. It didn't come with much luck, leaving us to live on one low income.

Dad's mental illness gradually grew worse. He stayed depressed and started seeing the "spirits" all the time. I was so scared that I didn't even want to watch a movie with the light off. I grew frightened of everything, and that fear started affecting me. I began experiencing my own demons from the corrupted environment in which I lived. I thought I saw shadows at night and felt like something was trying to get me. I was in an unknown spiritual warfare. I learned that when I prayed, it gave me peace and comfort. I began writing and singing to occupy my thoughts. It kept me from dwelling on the evil I felt in my home. Psalms 100:4–5 reads, "Enter his gates with thanksgiving, and his courts with praise; give thanks to him and praise his name. For the Lord is good and his love endures forever; his faithfulness continues through all generations."

At the time I didn't realize that what I was going through was preparing me to recognize the gifts of discernment God gave me. The situations led me to pray and seek him. Therefore, in doing so, I began looking at fear from a different perspective. I could literally feel people's hurt, addictions, and troubles. It's something that is hard to explain unless you have felt it yourself, but it's real! I hid all of this from everyone I knew because I didn't know what people would say. Honestly, I didn't know what it was myself or why I had these feelings. I have learned that every trial we go through is for a purpose, and that purpose is only found in Christ.

Moving forward, my parents decided to take a trip to a little holiness church my dad went to as a boy. They were excited for me to meet distant family I had never met. I didn't know what to expect! As we walked in the sanctuary, I felt a presence that was free, and the atmosphere was not like any other I had experienced before. The women had hair to their ankles, covered in long dresses, and no one wore makeup or jewelry. The men wore long-sleeved, button-down shirts, pants, and their beards were clean shaven. I felt a little out of place myself because I didn't look like them, but I felt embraced by their love.

The service began, and in the middle of it, I looked over and saw my dad praying. He wasn't just praying as he normally did, but this time there was a power behind his prayer. A man came from nowhere and laid his hands at the bottom of his spine. He was speaking in other tongues and rebuking Satan. My dad started throwing up what looked like green slime. Yes, green slime! They asked everyone to step back. They gathered around him and were praying like I had never seen before. I was a little nervous of what I was seeing before my eyes. This was my first real experience of seeing someone cast out demons. They kept saying, "Let go. Release it!" Shortly after, we noticed that the man who prayed for him was nowhere in sight, and no one knew who that man was! Matthew 12:28 states, "But if it is by the Spirit of God that I drive out demons, then the kingdom of God has come upon you."

On the way home, it was so quiet you could hear a pin drop. Dad made conversation first. He was talking to Mom and apologizing: "I'm sorry for everything I've put you through. Valerie, I love you!" She grinned and replied, "I love you, Mike!" I didn't want to talk. I just remained quiet. I was still trying to process what we experienced at that church. It was so unreal and more like the stuff you see in the movies. I looked at my dad completely differently, and I remember thinking there was something seriously wrong with him! That day was just the beginning of him being set free. There was still more that he had not released.

CHAPTER 4
A Living Nightmare

My ninth birthday had recently passed. The hopes for more structure and change in my family's situation, unfortunately, was still only a hope. Dad just could not shake this thing! For some reason, he continued to battle demonic forces. There were strongholds in my family and demonic oppression that Dad never fully surrendered. My home always got better for a while but never stayed that way. Mom and I stuck by Dad, and she stayed stressed, leading to emotional instability. She wasn't going to give up on him. If nothing else, I learned from her how to be strong! It wasn't long until my mom found out she was pregnant, and I was going to have another baby brother.

At this age, I still didn't sleep in my own bed and always slept between my parents. My mom and dad's relationship grew colder, and with Mom being pregnant, she slept on the couch in the living room. So I slept with my dad in the bed. Other than his loud, obnoxious snoring, nothing was out of the ordinary. I was a daddy's girl to say the least, so there was never an awkward moment. However, that began changing, and the enemy stole what little hope I had.

Late in the midnight hour, I was awakened to the one thing no child should experience. My dad had slipped his hand down my panties. I was frightened and still, as I was unsure of what to do! Was he allowed to do this to me? Is it wrong? I lay still and very quiet, as he massaged my privates. I was so confused and wondered if he thought I was Mom for some reason. When he was finished, I remember my mind was racing all over the place. Not understanding, I thought to myself, "It didn't hurt. Do I say anything? What if it was an accident?" I don't remember the dreary details of what I did next, as I was in a state of shock. But I do remember feeling dirty and empty.

As the sun showed its face, I got up, and dressed for school. My little girl parts were tingling, and it felt like a pulse beating. I recall sitting on the toilet and wiping myself with toilet paper several times to stop the tingle. When I applied pressure, it gave relief to the sensation. So I crumbled up a wad of toilet paper and placed it there. It was so hard for me not to show this humiliation on my face. I remember my dad acted completely normal that morning, and I guess I expected something different. Mom said, "Let's go, Baby, and I'll drop you off." My dad hugged me and told me to have a good day. I contemplated telling Mom on the way to school, but I just couldn't bring myself to do it. I was nervous. I was numb, and I was confused.

As I walked down the hallways of my school, I saw reality a little differently. I was quiet and observant, instead of my loud, silly self. I felt like everyone I passed was looking at me weird. I felt like they all knew what had happened just hours before. I couldn't focus on anything; I was in my own world. I was so afraid that the secret was going to get out, and I would be humiliated. I was so scared of all the wrong things, and I just wish I knew how to express myself. I wanted to be alone, and school was the last place that I wanted to be that morning.

Lunchtime approached and I sat at the table with my classmates. I didn't want anyone to sit close to me. I was so concerned they would notice I was having an off day and ask me questions. My paranoid behavior was so obvious, but no one took notice. Teachers, please take notice in your kids' personality changes. If someone would have talked to me, I may have been able to tell. No one, not one person even tried! I didn't even understand it myself! I remember I thought about playing sick, so I could call my mom to come get me, but I didn't. I battled it that entire day.

After school, I went to my granny Virgie's house as usual. My aunt Mary (my dad's sister) and my uncle Darwin were there. I was always excited to see them, and they made my day better. My mind was temporarily occupied, but the feeling was still there. Everyone said that my aunt Mary and I looked like we were mother and daughter. Before long, she adopted a baby boy, and their family was complete. She had her hands tied but never failed to treat me like more than a niece. My uncle Darwin said I was the apple of his eye, and he treated me as if I were his own.

Aunt Mary and I helped Granny fix dinner. We fixed what we called a "scrap dinner," and they were always the best dinners ever! Everything Granny could find we would cook. I would eat so much that I couldn't move. I have her to thank for all of my extra chubby love on my bones. She didn't just fix dinner but would fix dessert, too. I loved nothing more than spending my days with her, eating and watching my favorite television shows. However, sometimes I felt guilty for eating so much because she made a point to tell me I was getting too fat and needed to watch what I ate.

My insecurities grew, and I had a hard time accepting who I was. I don't blame her for it because I knew she wasn't being mean. It was just a concern that she had. However, those words hurt me, and I had issues with eating because of them. This is a lesson that sometimes even when we don't mean the things that we say, words can hurt. This brings me to this letter:

Dear Thick Women,
Love who you are, despite the negative words that were spoken over you! You are beautiful and look just as good in that bathing suit as the next person.

Do not feel like you have to look a certain way to be counted. My insecurities made me feel like I was not promoted at jobs because I didn't wear my suit as well as the skinny ladies. Crazy, right? Likewise, I felt that I wasn't good enough to play certain sports because I was on the heavier side. I carried this body image issue with everything that I did and didn't even notice. I tried diet after diet; my weight was up and down. I couldn't figure out what was wrong with me. I learned that dieting was my way to feel like I had control, but it was hurting me more than helping. Cut to the root of it and accept yourself for who you are. YOU ARE BEAUTIFUL IN EVERY WAY!! You were fearfully and wonderfully made in the image of Christ. If we all had that perfect body, what would the world look like? I love that we are different! So shine on, Sis, and do you!! The enemy has no room to mess with us because we are daughters of the King! I speak peace into your heart and mind right now! I declare and decree that you will love and forgive yourself. I claim VICTORY over the feeling of worthlessness, and prosperity in all that you do! It shall leave, and never return, in the NAME OF JESUS! AMEN!

Moving on, the sun went down, and the room grew silent. It was back to reality and facing the battles of my mind. I thought to myself, "Will it happen again? Would I do or say anything if it did? Surely, it was an accident!"

Once again, my mind was wandering everywhere. I could have stayed at Granny's that night, but I was curious if it would happen again. I wanted to know for myself if it was an accident or if my dad was this monster. I know it sounds crazy. I even questioned why I would go back, knowing that this happened. I went back because I didn't know any better. I had no knowledge of this, and I didn't understand it.

I went home and played in my room while Mom talked on the phone. This night was going to be different. I wanted to make sure I didn't fall asleep. I waited up, looking at the ceiling of my parent's room. A while passed, before my dad walked into the room and slid into the well sunken, floppy bed. I was so sleepy but fought the everlasting battle of closing my eyes. I turned my back to him, so he could not see my face. As the clock ticked, it took place once again. It was no longer a possibility for this to be an accident. It was really happening, and I loved him so much! I never imagined him doing this to me, and I made the choice not to tell.

Almost, every night following, he did the same things over and over. He never penetrated me, just fondled me. Unfortunately, I never told anyone and wasn't brave enough to try. I grew used to the throb, the tickle, and the swelling. Sadly, I began to like the sensation, and that made it even worse. Sometimes, I would even watch dirty television shows on the late night Cinemax, trying to understand what this feeling was about. I became fond of feeling like I was a woman, and I wanted to look like the beautiful, naked women in the movies. I grew up way too fast, and I went from playing princess to watching porn in a short time.

A long year passed. My dad woke up really early one morning and went into the kitchen. He seemed very bothered that morning. I'll never forget his uneasy body language. I had gone into the kitchen looking for breakfast, and he blurted, "Tabby you can't sleep with me anymore. You're getting too old to be in bed with me." I was taken by surprise to hear him say that. I had feelings of embarrassment, anger, and confusion. Why would he suddenly say that after this long? Did he feel conviction? Guilt? What was it? I remember thinking, "He is going to tell Mom, and my life is over." I walked away and went to my room, only saying, "OK," waiting for the reason to reveal itself. However, nothing happened, and I know now that it was conviction. Now this is a note that God has ordained me to write to every predator out there:

Dear Predator,

If you are sitting in a jail cell or simply been given mercy for your wrong doings, know that God loves you. He is not pleased with your actions but will deliver you! For Christ died for all sins, even yours. Maybe you were a victim yourself, and that curse led you to repeating the same actions. As much as I am disgusted as a victim, I know that God loves and does so unconditionally. If you are reading this, this is your open invitation to surrender your life, con-

fess your sins, and REPENT! In doing so, and for the right reasons, you shall be delivered! I speak the power of the Holy Spirit to manifest in your mind, heart, and soul RIGHT NOW. I speak conviction into your heart, and every demonic force to be cast down RIGHT NOW and not return, in the name of JESUS CHRIST, our Lord and Savior. You will not touch another child. You will not have the thoughts of touching another child. You will not find pleasure in pornography, and you will be freed from the sickness that resonates in your mind! Under the sound of my voice, YOU SHALL BE HEALED!!!! Lastly, I ask that you go to your victim and sincerely apologize. Let them know that you are ashamed of what you have done, and give God the Glory for freedom in your mind. They deserve your apology because now they have to live with this for the rest of their lives. Their pain is not in vain!! Give them the freedom they deserve! And it shall be done!

CHAPTER 5
Acting Out

After beginning middle school, Mom had my brother in late September, and I was so happy. I believe Mom and Dad were on better terms once my brother was born. Dad had straightened up some, and I am sure it helped them cope with the hurt from my brother who passed eight years before. I had a lot of problems at this point. I played boyfriend/girlfriend with my dolls. I learned to masturbate and continued watching porn every chance I got. I developed very bad habits from the molestation, and it controlled every aspect of my mind.

I went to the neighborhood park to hang out with some of the older kids who played ball there. Of course, it was cold and at that time I didn't stay out long. Some boys who played there were older and a couple of grades up from me. I was a little shy but enjoyed every minute of their attention. I had just hit the puberty stage and found myself attracted to them. I had no knowledge of saving myself until I was married or of any morals for that matter.

Before long, I allowed one of the boys to touch me and play with my privates. I would go to the park just to see them every day. Although I was a virgin, I was used to the sensation of being touched and wanted more. Likewise, I had girls who were my friends, and we played boyfriend/girlfriend every weekend. I guess you could say I just liked the feeling of being sexual. I was afraid of going all the way because I didn't want to become pregnant. I was still a kid myself. If not for that fear, I probably would have lost my virginity very young.

The boys from the park began going around school saying I was easy. I was so mad, and angry because it ruined my reputation. I didn't want the other kids knowing my secrets! I began lying and telling everyone it wasn't true!!! I couldn't lose what little bit of normalcy I had, and it was already a struggle for me to trust. I quit going to the park for this reason, and I drew my attention more to the girls I was intimate with. This led to my identity crisis and questioning who I was.

With the girls, it was always awkward to start kissing or touching each other. We would watch a dirty movie or take a bubble bath to lead us into the comfort of sexual activities. I was never allowed to stay at anyone's house, and so they came to mine. We became fond of pleasuring each other. To be so young, we were fully intimate and had no clue that what we were doing. It would haunt us for the rest of our lives.

I think a couple of these girls lost their virginity before middle school. Surprisingly, for the longest time I thought it was just me who had a burning desire. It was enjoyable for a little while but when I noticed the "pretty" girls in school getting boyfriends and holding hands in the hallway, I wanted the same thing. My self-esteem was low because of my deep dark secrets. So finding a good guy wasn't going to be easy. I grew tired of being who I was and what I was doing.

The summer of 2000 began, and I had the best time of my life. My best friend lived on a drive in, and I stayed with her all the time. Her lifestyle was the life I longed for because she was loved. Her mom would take her places and support her in sports, and she was all around fun. Actually, my mom and her mom were best friends. That entire summer, we were together every day and made memories for a lifetime.

My friend was dating this boy whose grandparents were very wealthy. We would go to their house and swim in their pool all the time. Soon, I met a boy named Bentley, and he was my summer boyfriend. My favorite thing to do was sing and dance. We were always entertaining each other and actually being kids. This was the one time in my life that I felt like I had a life. It only lasted for a summer, but it was one I would never forget.

I began eighth grade in August 2001. Things began looking up for me, and I met a guy who was the captain of the football team. His name was Bradley, and he was different from the other guys. He was very kind, smart, and a total gentleman. He was tall and perfectly built with blonde hair and blue eyes. We flirted in the hallways and soon began dating. He was my first real boyfriend. My reputation grew by being with him because he was a good guy who had his life together. I attended all of his games, I wore his football jacket and looked forward to seeing him every day. With him, I found my temporary normal, and it felt so good.

My parents moved into an apartment complex in town, and they wanted to save money. Bradley and his mom picked me up every Saturday at 4:00, and I would go to his house for dinner. We would sit at the top of a mountainside until dark and talk about our dreams and how much we cared for one another. It was several months before we even kissed. He didn't know anything about my sexual desires or my secrets; I would never tell him. He wouldn't have understood, and he would have broken up with me.

Bradley and I had dated for seven months before I started talking to an older guy who was in the 11th grade. He lived in the townhouse apartment next to mine. He was more of what I felt I deserved—the bad boy. I broke it off with Bradley and never looked back. I recall us having a conversation about sex, and I told him I wasn't a virgin. This conversation happened when he came to my house, and we pulled up the notepad on my computer to chat quietly.

For me, Johnny was amazingly irresistible! His dark hair, tanned skin, and green eyes made me melt. His smile was contagious, and his personality was full of surprises. In our conversation, we talked about what we liked as far as sex. He then proceeded to tell me, "I want you!" Smiling inside, I wanted him, too, and I felt ready! This is the guy I will give it to. He was the one! That night, I snuck out of my house and came in his back door. He was waiting! His house smelled like the Glade Hawaiian Paradise. I was so nervous and it definitely showed, but he had a way to ease my thoughts. However, it wasn't long before he noticed I was fidgeting and questioned if I were ready. There was no way that I wasn't going through with this, and my mind was made up.

Johnny caressed my body and told me he was going to take care of me. Everything a girl wanted to hear, he said it. He began the deed, and I scooted across the floor. It hurt so badly! No one had told me this was painful. "Why is this so painful?" I thought to myself.

He asked," Are you OK?" I nodded my head and he continued. I couldn't enjoy it for a little while. I hated it! He kept stopping and staring down at me. "Are you sure you're not a virgin?"

"YES, oh my God just do it." He could see how uncomfortable I was, so he stopped and that's when he noticed I lied to him.

"You were a virgin. Why would you lie to me? I mean, that's a good thing. Why didn't you just tell me?" I started to cry in embarrassment. I didn't even know that females bleed when they have sex for the first time.

I was a child who thought I knew about life because I was molested.

Dear Parents,
Please talk to your preteens and let them know what this stuff is. Make them aware and let them know that it's not at all what it is made out to be. Tell them the importance of saving their virginity for marriage. I felt disgusted and realized that I had no clue what in the world I was doing. I wish that my mother would have been comfortable talking to me about this stuff. Of course, I took sexual education class, but that in no way prepared me for this. Invest in them and teach them all that you can. Who knows, this may prevent them from making wrong choices. I understand these conversations are not easy, but they are necessary. Let them be comfortable talking to you, so they don't hide things from you. I pray that God gives you the words to say, the strength to say it, and the ability to monitor it. I pray that your child does not give up their purity, and that they will never suffer this kind of shame. Amen!

School was out and my summer before high school was soon going to begin. I started hanging out with Johnny more and riding around the neighborhood with him. We never had a relationship, other than friends with benefits. We began falling apart when he told some high schoolers in our complex that we had sex. I was mad!!!

Once again another low life guy had to break my trust! He had a one-night stand with a girl I called a best friend at the time. I was envious and fought her in the parking lot of the apartments. I beat her up pretty badly because I blamed her for what happened. I knew I was wrong for how it happened, but I didn't have any remorse.

I started talking to different people and grew comfortable in having sex with different guys. None of them were in my age range, and I just acted out of hurt. I just wanted to be wanted and loved! While searching for love in all the wrong places, I earned the name of a whore. Being as pretty as I was, I did not know my worth. Here I was, labeled a whore before I even knew what a whore was. When my dad caught on to what I was doing, he called me a "whore and slut" when he was angry! I owned it, and I was convinced that I was that label. My clothing included short shorts, low-cut tops, and thongs sticking out of my pants. I wanted men to look at me, and I craved their attention. Sadly, that was what happened, and I was put in situations that I was not strong enough to get out of.

CHAPTER 6

No Place to Turn

I became lost in my corrupted ways. I started drinking alcohol, snorting pain pills, and smoking weed. It felt good to get away from my own mind. I never had a problem getting it because of the people I was hanging around. A lady who was paralyzed from the waist down, in a wheelchair, by the name of Carla had all the parties at her place. She supplied me with anything I wanted. She lived in the apartment complex next to mine, and so I stayed there a lot. She lived by herself, and she enjoyed the company. Therefore, everyone would use her for her pills.

I met a guy who always did "runs" for her. There was a time or two before when I saw him walking around the complex with his friend. He was 23 years old at the time, and to this day I couldn't tell you why in the world I thought he hung the moon. I found him very attractive! Carla introduced Koda to me, and we immediately hit it off. Although I was so young, he didn't seem to be bothered by it. He did ask me if my parents cared whether I dated older guys. I giggled and said, "They don't keep up with nothing I do, and you don't have anything to be concerned about." That's where our rollercoaster of a relationship began, and my life forever changed.

Koda and his friend, David, would always meet me and my friends at Carla's house in the evening. We stayed high and snorted pills until it was time for me to go home. He always made sexual gestures towards me and was smooth with his words. I made him wait a while because I was tired of giving it out and not having anything to show for it. I wanted to get to know him first to make sure he wasn't going to do to me as the others had done. He was very anxious and impatient but waited. After a short couple of months, we had sex for the first time, and I was trapped in a serious situation.

Summer was almost over. I was doing pills every day and was on my way to becoming an alcoholic. I didn't care about anything or anyone. I looked forward to my days with Koda and the adventures that came with him. He was changing me, and I was being swallowed up into his games. I was completely blindsided by reality, and only cared about him. I started hanging around the apartments with a group of people who were disconnected from reality. They called themselves the "Crips." I thought they were tough, people I could identify with, and I connected with their lifestyle. I was drawn to their independence and ability to fear nothing. So I thought it was cool to be around them and felt empowered by making bad choices.

I was a complete mess, and everyone I used to call a friend wanted nothing to do with me. I thought I was cute, and no one could control me. I was full of pride, and I had a toxic personality. I would fight girls for no reason just to prove that I wasn't one to be messed with. I was suspended a lot and stayed in ISD (in school detention). That's what I wanted anyways because I hated everyone, especially myself. I was so confused and lost in a world of darkness.

The fighting, drugs, and alcohol got out of control. On my birthday, August 29, 2002, my parents sent me to the same place my dad went years before—Charter Ridge. I knew that it wasn't going to help me because I did not want help. I called Koda several times while I was in there just to hear him say he was waiting on me. While there, they diagnosed me with oppositional–defiant disorder and impulsive control disorder. My charts actually made me look like I didn't belong there because I was good at manipulating the counselors.

The days seemed so long. I begged my mom to get me out. Every day was the same routine: wake up, take medications, eat breakfast, go to group activities, do school work, have gym time, eat dinner, shower, and go to bed. They watched me sleep throughout the night to see if I had any abnormal habits. I wasn't dumb. I knew how to beat their system. There were people there who were literally crazy, and I didn't feel that I belonged. I wasn't like them.

Mom felt bad for me being there and was happy to see me when I was released. I told her, "I'm never doing that stuff again, and I learned my lesson." Truth was, that was all a lie, and I just wanted to get back into my comfortable lifestyle. As soon as we got home, I was back at it. This time I was given a 10:00 pm curfew. I had plenty of time to do what I wanted and still didn't care if I was late.

Word got out that Koda was back with his "baby momma!" I didn't even know he had one at the time! It turned out he was a living lie himself. I was devastated because my life revolved around him. I mentally broke down, and I didn't want to live anymore. How could he betray me like that? I didn't see it coming. I guess I was too stuck on trying to be grown up, and I failed to realize what comes with that choice.

Late one evening, right after the sun went down, I was walking through the apartment complex. A guy named Neil was sitting on a stairwell outside. He was a jerk, and everyone knew him. He walked like he was a "Big Dog," and he thought he was a king! Honestly, I hated even to look at him. He said," Come here!" I walked over his way. His eyes looked evil, and he was biting his lip. He said, "I hear you've been giving it out?"

"No," I replied.

"Yeah you do. Don't play that bull with me."

Nervously, I went to turn around, and he grabbed my arm in a tight grip. I shouted, "Let go of me!" He eased his grip but still held my arm. His brother and two other guys came around the corner of the building. I knew them and didn't think they were bad guys.

He convinced me to walk in the laundry room connected to the building. They followed and shut the door. He sat up on a metal folding table and said, "Suck me!" I gagged and almost puked. The smell of his privates was disgusting. The guys just watched, as I nervously tried to avoid his request. I was scared and nervous. He grabbed my hair and locked his hand in it. "I said suck it!" He forced my head down and put it in my mouth. The guys didn't see what happened before they came around that corner. I knew that this was perceived to be something, it wasn't. I did not want to do anything with this guy, and they were unknowingly witnessing sexual assault.

A noise hit the laundry room door. He jumped up, and the door busted open. It was Johnny!! He must have heard what was going on, and Neil pulled his pants up quick. I took off running to my house. I felt disgusted and ashamed. I was scared and didn't want anyone to find out, but it got out quick. I returned to school, and although he didn't go to my school, his brother did. That's when the name calling and harassment began.

I finally got to where I couldn't take any more and I turned him in. I went to my counselor's office and asked for help. I didn't even want to go back home. I knew I couldn't show my face outside. My counselor called my mom and told her everything. My mom was upset that I didn't come to her and wanted him prosecuted. I just wanted to die! I didn't want any part of what was going to take place. I would have never said anything had it not been for the embarrassment I had to face in school.

Cops questioned him and the other guys. After several court dates, I believe, he was placed on house arrest. I know that he moved from town shortly after. I stayed low key for a while and drank all the time. The local bootlegger knew me well! After it died down a little, Koda returned into the picture. He said he wanted to hook back up. I wanted to feel some sort of love, somehow! I felt like I had no place to turn! I accepted his petty plea and we were back on again. I had no respect for myself and couldn't care less at that point. I just wanted to feel something normal and he was that normal for me.

CHAPTER 7
Gone Too Far

I started hanging around the apartments with a group of people who were disconnected from reality. My addiction was on a whole new level. I felt the urge to snort painkillers—morning, noon, night, and in-between. I was destroyed, worthless, and broken. My parents couldn't control me, and no one could help me. I was so far out there, I didn't see myself coming back. I didn't know who I was anymore. Honestly, I didn't care! I lived in the misery of my own mind. If you were around me and had something that I could take, I would've taken it without question. That was my mind-set, and I never thought I would change.

This is a part of my story that I wasn't going to share, but I know that I have to. God told me to hold nothing back, and this was the only thing that I wanted to hold. The shame of my father molesting me was bad enough but there was another situation that I was even more ashamed of. My mom doesn't even know this happened;

this was my best-kept secret. There was another relative who preyed on my weakness, and he followed through with getting me messed up and penetrating me. Now, I write this letter to you:

Dear Relative,

As I began writing my story, I was going to leave this part out but it was meant for me to share. I knew when you caught wind of this book that you would search for your name or this story. Yeah, it had to be released, too. I know that you to had something happen when you were young that led to your issues. Still to this day, you are lost and doing the same things you did in high school. A girl who had relations with you told me how bad you hurt her and that she was seriously scared of you. I hid from you for the longest time because when I looked at you I felt shame. However, I want you to know that I forgive you, and most of all I forgive myself. I still want nothing to do with you, but I pray that you allow God to heal your heart. I pray that he completely transforms your mind and that you are delivered from your ways. After this day, you will no longer be attached to me, and you will be set free. I am speaking into your life, just as I am called to do for others. BE SET FREE, IN THE NAME OF JESUS!! This generational curse is no more, and it stops now. You will not touch another young girl. You will not be a weapon for the enemy to use, and you will be changed, in Jesus' name. Amen!

Now, high school parties got a little wild! I attended all of them that I could get invited to. I was usually always naked and dancing on a table before midnight. I didn't care who was there and what I was drinking. The only thing that mattered was getting hammered and numbing my painful reality. My mom always threatened to snitch on whoever I was hanging with if I was caught at a party. I didn't let that stop me. There was nothing more she could do. I manipulated everyone and didn't care whom I hurt. My brother was a toddler at this point, and I knew she had to focus on his needs. So I just did what I wanted and forgot the rest.

Around 2:30 in the morning, on a cold winter night, I found myself naked and digging my fingernails in the cold ground of a ditch. Koda and I had split up for like the fifth time in a year. Every time we broke up, I would go on a binge to get out of my head. This night, in particular, I was in a ditch line at Powell's Village Apartment complex. I didn't live there, but some people I was partying with did. To this day, I don't know what happened or why I was in the ditch. I experienced something supernatural. I heard a voice say, "Get up! You're not dying here!" No one was around me at the time. I rolled over and couldn't stand up. I remember lying there and thinking I was about to die.

"Help me! Help me!" I muttered. "God help me!!" My speech was drawn and my vision was doubled. I felt my life leaving my body. I slowly raised my head and my phone was beside me. The fog of the streetlights blinded me. Some people recognized me and ran over in my direction. I couldn't see who they were; I just passed out. I have no recollection of anything!! It was lights out from there. I woke up in Koda's bed, and I didn't know how I got there. I was a hot mess that morning, and I rushed home to get cleaned up.

That night, I went to Carla's house and got wasted again. I was so trashed, and I went too far. Two girls I knew dragged me over to my parents' house. My mom was at work and Dad wasn't home. I was throwing up everywhere before passing completely out. They were left with no choice but to get me help. They called my mom and everyone rushed to the house.

My mom called my entire family to come to the house. My aunt, my cousin, and everybody! They put me in a bathtub and poured cold water over me. I had little feeling and couldn't function at all. My body was lifeless, but I was mumbling stupid talk. That's when they called an ambulance and had me transported to the hospital. I was unconscious and do not remember any part of getting there.

I don't know how much time had passed, but I faintly woke up to bright lights in my eyes and my family standing around me. The doctor came in. He began checking my vitals and talking to my parents. When I fully gained my body back, he informed me I was lucky to be alive! I had so much drugs and alcohol in my body, I should have been dead! I was too young to have this kind of problem. He followed by telling Mom he recommended getting me help. If not, my parents needed to send me to juvenile detention. I needed help with my addiction and the people I chose to associate with.

My mom was disappointed in me. I could see the anger and hurt in her eyes. The next morning, she brought me home to pack my bags and say my goodbyes. Once again, I was going to the same location as before. I thought about running away before we left because I knew that this time she wouldn't be able to come get me out. It was a no-win situation. I was going to have to complete the treatment. I was so tired of dealing with this stuff. I just wanted to be left alone, but the choice wasn't mine to make.

Dear Addict,

I write this from a sincere heart and understanding. I know that life is hard, and I know that it only takes one time to get hooked. Do not let the drugs or alcohol take your life from you. Do not let them steal your joy any longer. Whatever led you to it, God can get you through it. Believe that he will do it RIGHT NOW!!! I cast down every stronghold of addiction and every battle in the mind! I pray that as you read this, the taste for it is taken from your mouth. You will no longer be bound by this addiction. For you shall be delivered and set free. In the mighty name of Jesus! Amen!! Remember, all you have to do is believe this and have faith that it is done!

My mom pulled up to the rehab center on December 8th, and I got out. She signed me in and briefly explained why I needed help. This was doctor ordered, so I had to stay. They put me through the evaluation phase and showed me my room. There were rules that I didn't want to follow, but knew if I wanted out early, I had to. Some of those rules were getting up at 7:00 am, making my bed, going to breakfast, and going to class. I still had to complete school stuff while in there. It was a lot different from my normal work and super easy. However, I didn't want to do anything but sleep.

I did as they asked and began my treatment. Over the next few days, I experienced withdrawal from the drugs and alcohol. I was very irritable and had an upset stomach and sweats. They put me on some kind of antidepressant and said it would help me with the anxiety. I had extreme highs and the lowest lows on this medicine. I always wanted to go to the gym for free time. I would do leg presses and bench weights to relieve my anger. That was the only thing that kept my sanity in that place. My diagnosis this time was a list of things: Conduct disorder, mood disorder, oppositional–defiant disorder, polysubstance abuse, and alcohol abuse.

This time treatment was more extensive than before. It gave me a little hope, but I still did not have confidence that I was going to do the right things when discharged. I knew I still had desires to continue the same things as before. I guess I tried to lie to myself and make believe I was better. I didn't know who I was, and I never really knew. To say that I was just going to change was not realistic. This was a lifestyle for me, and I didn't know anything different. Other people weren't going to see me as a changed person, so why should I? I didn't have worth and worried about all the things that I shouldn't have been concerned about. For me to be so tough, that was my weakness!

After I was released, I stayed in for a couple days and tried to resist the urge. I couldn't do it much longer. My dad was my trigger. He didn't know how to keep his mouth off of me and would make me angry. When mad at me for something, he would say, "You're never going to amount to anything at the rate you're going!" I was always the blame for ruining our family and perfect image! I was the one who didn't have enough sense to do what I was supposed to. I was only worried about boys and booze!

Yeah, a lot of that was true. He was right! All I ever wanted to say was, "You made me this way!" Oh how I wished I could tell it all! I didn't though. I was so far gone that no one would have believed me.

It didn't take long for me to get back with Koda and back to the drugs. I was a sophomore in high school and was nothing like the others. I was hanging out with older people and built my own life outside of school. My parents knew I was back at it, but I manipulated them into believing I was OK, and wouldn't take it overboard like before. I made myself believe that I had control of my addiction.

Once again, my anxiety and depression became unbearable. I started cutting myself to relieve the pain. I
would slice my arm just enough to feel numb. I never
went deep enough to have permanent scars but enough
for temporary marks. I enjoyed the sting, as it gave me
relief. Everyone wanted to fight me because my mouth
always caused drama. I felt hopeless and worthless! The
drugs, the alcohol, and the cutting didn't numb me long.
Reality was always there when it was time to come down.

I came in late one night with some weed on me. My
dad started questioning me because my eyes were blood-
shot. He snatched the bag out of my purse and talked
down to me. The cops were called and they came in
questioning me. I was told how disrespectful I was and
all the things that they could do to me for having drugs
in my possession. I took it with a grain of salt and had
no interest in their words. My parents thought they were
going to put some kind of fear in me, but I didn't fear the
police. They took me into the station as a scare tactic and
ended up doing nothing.

I was battling demons and at my complete breaking
point. I am not sure what led to the tragic moment that
was about to take place, but I do remember I was at rock
bottom. I went into my parents' bedroom with an ivory
flower crown that is used for flower girls in a wedding.
I put it around my neck tightly and hung it to their closet doorknob. I was ready to die and forget it all! That's
when my baby brother walked in, screaming and crying.
I struggled to pull the headpiece off and got it right in

time. I sat there, dizzy and seeing stars. I'll never forget that feeling. Mom came running and immediately freaked out. My lips were turning blue and my face was that dark red/purple color. Without a doubt, I was almost dead! My mom lost all control, and I remember the look in her eyes. I was at death's door, and so was she from the hurt it caused.

Days later, I found a new friend, and we met at a local wrestling show. Her name was Janice. She was known for snorting pills, and we hung out every weekend. She drove a white Malibu, and I was always riding with her because I wasn't of age to drive, so she would pick me up to go out. Every weekend was a new adventure with different guys. We would go to adult parties in Lexington and run the roads. Janice and I had a lot in common, and I looked up to her.

We were very lucky that we didn't die on some of our trips. There was never a moment that we weren't high. However, there was one trip, in particular, that I'll share here. She introduced me to some friends of hers—two guys from Mount Sterling whom I did not know. They had the connections for the good stuff. They were smoking crack from a pipe, which was not something that I had ever done. This was my first time being introduced to rocks, and it was a high I will never forget.

We smoked so much and went on a run to Lexington to get more drugs. The guy who was in the back seat with me kept staring at me, winking his eye, and rubbing my arm. He passed me the pipe and taught me how to take a hit from it. It was like I was in another world, and my senses were so intense. After a couple of hits, I was down for whatever with no strings attached. This high was not like the others; it took me to space.

We ended up making two runs to Lexington that night and crashing at his house after. A lot happened, and some stuff I don't even remember. However, I did remember that this was on a Sunday night, and I was supposed to be at school the next morning when I woke up. There was no way that I could go because I was coming down off of an extreme high. I had my friend call and act like my mom, so they would not call her. Somehow, it worked, and I didn't go back home until that night.

Of course, my mom was used to me staying out, and she got tired of me lying all the time. She tried to keep me from it, but I always found a way to do what I wanted. I had a relative who wanted to hang out, and I guess Mom felt comfort in me doing things with her. What Mom didn't realize is that she was a whore and got me into a lot of trouble. This relative slept with any- and everyone. She really liked the older men and tried finding love in all the wrong places.

She took me to hang out with some friends of hers, and we drank. No drugs that night, only drinking. However, there were several guys in the house and only us two girls. She went to have sex with her boyfriend at the time, and I believe to this day that something was slipped in my beer. I remember this guy taking me into a room. I was halfway unconscious, and he raped me. I woke up to no one around, and my family member was missing. I had no choice but to call my mom so that I could get a ride home. Once again, I was left with no one and felt worthless.

I never told a soul about the rape, and I kept it to myself. I had so much happen to me that I felt I deserved it. I felt that I was cursed, and bad things were always going to happen. There was one last time that I went out with that relative, and she was the one who got raped. Sadly, I had to call my mom that night, too, to pick me up in Wolfe County. I had no clue where I was, and I was scared. I remember having to lock myself in a bathroom to try and get cell service because I was so far out.

Shortly after this chain of traumatic events, Mom sent me to my aunt Mary's house to live in hope that I would change my ways. Their home was very structured, and I respected them more than anyone else. There were rules I had no choice but to follow. Aunt Mary would sit and talk to me about what I was feeling and help me cope with it any way possible. I enjoyed feeling like I was important and inspired to change my ways. She took me to school in the morning and brought me home in the evening. There was no going out, and homework was a priority. I was getting used to it, but I still had connections at school to buy painkillers, when needed. On the weekends, when I went to visit my parents, I took advantage of it. Slowly, things began to change for me.

CHAPTER 8

Getting to Know God

I was used to partying every weekend, but one particular Friday night that changed. My mom asked me, "Tab, will you go to church with me?" She explained how much I was going to love it and how the preacher may be able to help me. "They are different!" she said. I had no intentions of going! I didn't trust people in the church, and I definitely didn't trust the preachers in the church. You may ask yourself, "Why?" Here's your answer: I had already had a bad name at that church because I dated two brothers at different times, and I was hated. Second, due to being molested by my father, I lost all trust in the church. Third, I believed in God but for some reason I thought he hated me. I was so bad that I thought I would never be able to change. My life was cursed, and there was no changing that.

After my mother begged, I said, "There is only one way I will go. I have to bring a friend with me!" She agreed, and that following Sunday evening we were on our way to church. I took some "meds" before going. I was only going so she would be happy. I didn't care what those people thought of me. I wore skintight jeans that showed the lining of my bottom, a hoodie, and my famous big hoop earrings. They were not appealing to these types of religious folk, but I wasn't trying to fit in anyway. I'm sure to them I looked as if I "came off the nearest corner."

The sun was down and the evening sky went black. We pulled up to the small, white country church in Irvine, Kentucky. My mom was excited and talked the whole way there. I believe she felt this was the last chance to get me help. My friend Marcy and I sat in the back seat. We were laughing and giggling before the service started. Church members was shaking our hands and telling us, "It's so nice to have you join us." I felt so out of place, but they didn't judge me like I thought they would. Either they were being fake or they were happy to see me.

The doors to the church foyer came open. In walked this family, and they were all dressed in nice suits and shiny shoes. The pastor, first lady, their three sons, and daughter walked straight to the pulpit. My heart began fluttering so hard that I could literally hear it. One of their boys got on the piano and began to play softly and sing. His voice was like angels singing! A feeling came over me that I had never experienced before. I looked over at Marcy and said, "He's the one!!" She looked at me as if I were crazy!! I was dead serious though. I know that is almost unbelievable, but I knew he was sent to me. I just knew he was one of my purposes for being there. I didn't know why and I didn't care. All I wanted to know was who this guy was! He definitely wasn't the type I'd typically go for. I liked the bad boys, but I couldn't shake the feeling.

After service was over, we made eye contact, but he never walked my way. I was bummed and didn't want it to be obvious. All the way home, my mom and Marcy kept poking fun about my secret crush. Mom said, "See, if you wouldn't have come tonight, you wouldn't have even known he existed. I have to be honest with you though. I can't see you two together." Her saying that made me want him that much more. I mean at this point all the negatives in my life were getting a little overwhelming. I was tired of hearing what I couldn't do, how much I had screwed up, and what is going to end up happening! I longed for positivity somewhere.

My aunt Melinda was on the praise team at church and asked me to come back that next Sunday. I chose not to go and instead partied at the neighbors. She called me right after it was over and said, "The nice looking guy that played piano asked about you and told me he would like to see you again." I couldn't believe it!! He really noticed me!! I tried to play like I didn't care, but deep inside I was ecstatic!! With that being said, I did attend the week after. I brought Marcy back with me and what took place was unbelievable.

Once again, I was mesmerized by the voice that came from behind the keys. The preacher stood up to bring forth the word God gave him. Upon praying he called me to the altar. I was in shock at first and nervous to say the least. I had heard about how he was a prophet and a real man of God. I was thinking to myself, "He's going to call me out and his son will never talk to me." I hesitated and went to the front. I was by no means prepared for what was about to take place.

The anointed preacher got a bottle of blessed oil and placed his oily hands on top of my head. As he began praying in the Spirit, I closed my eyes. He began rebuking every stronghold, every addiction, and every temptation from my mind!! He spoke Life over me! I felt hands all around me. It took what seemed like forever to pray over me. He kept saying," Accept it!! Release it! God is knocking at your heart! You are chosen!" I didn't know what was happening, but I felt light as a feather! I couldn't stand and hit the hard floor. I was out of it, just like the night I was unconscious going to the hospital! This night God began his work on my life.

As I lay on the floor, I heard a still, small voice speak to my heart! The same voice that spoke to me when I lay in the ditch line, helpless, on that wasted night. It was the voice of God! "Walk upright in my will and I will heal thee! It's not over until I say it's over!" I began shaking uncontrollably. I opened my eyes and couldn't move! People were standing over me, and I was stuck like glue to the floor. They went to help me up, and that's when I found myself drunk. Not off a bottle of Jim Beam but from a new wine that God was pouring over me.

After the God-ordained service was over, Shaun, the piano player, walked my way. He said, "I'm glad you got in the service tonight. I'm even happier you came back!" I just smiled, and after a short talk we exchanged numbers. He was just one of two purposes for me attending that service! God used him to bring me back and give me hope and a desire for a better life. He knew exactly what he was doing. I slowly began to see that it wasn't that God didn't love me. It was me not loving myself.

CHAPTER 9
Leaving My Past

I was so swallowed up in my negative life that I didn't know how to change. Shaun helped me in my process. We grew close to each other, and he was so wise for his age. Our friendship wasn't easy because we lived over an hour apart. The first thing I did after coming home from school was to call him. Just hearing his voice was motivation for me to try another day. My addiction slowly got better but my self-image was a work in progress. That's when I came to realize I had a lot to change.

I had a guy friend whom I had known for several years. His name was Darren. We had a secret relationship that was different from all the others. I cheated behind the back of every guy whom I had dated with Darren. Darren and I were so much alike that we knew we couldn't be an item, so we stayed "friends with benefits." Our toxic relationship was more of a fantasy. He was captain of a basketball team and a hustler on the side.

He would pick me up from any party I was at and let me stay with him until I sobered up. He helped me so many times with what I was going through. I secretly wanted a relationship with him, but I knew that it wouldn't work. If he wanted one then he would tell me, but he wasn't that type to have strings attached. So I accepted that and didn't seek more.

When Shaun and I started becoming serious, I spent the night with Darren one last time. I knew I had to let him know that our fantasy relationship was going to have to stop. I did just that and he didn't accept it like I thought he would. He said, "I thought we promised each other, no matter what happens we will always see each other?" That is a promise we did make but that was before I really found the right guy for me. As much as I wanted to continue seeing him, I knew I would hurt them both. So I had to let go of one, and I wanted to do what was right for once in my life.

Darren showed a little emotion by the things he said, and I questioned if I was doing the right thing. I thought about all the girls he had calling him, and I knew that this was an illusion in my head. He couldn't leave that life and be faithful to just one girl. So, as hard as it was, I said my goodbyes. I knew that something better awaited, and for me to receive it, I had to change my ways.

Not long after, Shaun and I began having problems. He said he didn't want a girl like me. He wanted someone who was classy and respected herself. I was so hurt and angry that he waited to let me down like that. The church people gossiped about me all the time. They didn't want us together, so I blamed them for his sudden change of perception. He grew frustrated with me and didn't want me to call him anymore. I finally stepped back and let him be. I was sad but didn't show it.

I quit going to church and moved back in with my parents. I slowed down partying and found some hope in my life to do better for myself. I attended after-school programs. I began writing poetry more and keeping myself busy. I hung out with guy friends but I didn't pursue any more relationships. I was hoping Shaun would see what he gave up! I knew I needed to work on me because I couldn't love anyone else without loving myself first.

In my process of change, I went through so many emotions. I didn't know which way to turn. The friends I had were gone. The relationships I had were done, and my life was a sinkhole. I had hit rock bottom once again. Only this time, I knew I could rise from it because I did find hope in Christ. I kept faith. I had a desire to change and began praying for God to help me. I needed to learn how to love the right way. I needed to learn respect for myself, and I needed to learn to let my past go. Those three things were the hardest to do in my life. I knew I couldn't do it alone, so I surrendered.

Soon after my junior prom, I got my license and began driving. Getting out of my parents' house helped me cope. Taking long drives through the mountains and back roads allowed me to clear my head. I was so mad that I could finally drive, and Shaun no longer talked to me. I just continued doing me and focused on my future. I worked at my granny's restaurant every day to put back money and save up to leave the cursed town I lived in.

My last year as a high school student approached! No one imagined I'd even graduate, so I was going to make sure I proved them all wrong. I worked super hard to keep my grades up and attend school regularly. I quit fighting, I only partied on occasion, and I still took pain-killers privately. I guess I should just say I didn't go looking for the drugs like before, but I took them any-time they were around. I was much better than the previous year. I was moving forward instead of backwards.

Sitting at the lunchroom table at school, my friend Marcy randomly brought up Shaun. She told some of her friends about the church and her experience. It had been about five months since I talked to him. Hearing his name still made me feel butterflies in my stomach. She said I should call him again. I just wasn't sure that I wanted to be the one to call first. So she took it upon herself to call for me. "Remember what you said? He's the one? Right?"

"Yeah, sure!" I replied sarcastically.

I stood anxiously while she dialed his number. I just knew he wasn't going to answer. We were in school! I mean what were the odds of him not being in class? She was smiling and began talking over the phone. He actually picked up! She began telling him how good I was doing now and how we should all meet up and hang out. Before, we only saw each other at church, so really we didn't have a social life outside those four walls. He agreed, and we planned to meet. She said, "Piece of cake! Girl, don't give up. He's a good guy!" Just like that, I was ready for the weekend. I couldn't wait to see him once again.

The school week passed slowly, and I had planned every detail for the weekend. Shaun called me a couple times and told me he missed our conversations. He opened up to me about some things he had gone through, and once again that spark relit in our friendship. I didn't even try hard. This time I wanted him to get to know the real me, not the illusion of who I tried to be. I knew if it were going to work, then it was going to have to be real and nothing fake.

That Friday the bell rang and Marcy and I met at the gym doors. We discussed our plan and went home to get ready. I picked her up and we left town. I had never driven that far and never driven on the Interstate. I didn't even care. I put the pedal to the metal and went! Once we arrived in his area, I called him, and he gave me directions to his house. We pulled up, and I was so nauseous I thought I was going to barf. Luckily, I contained myself and acted like I was all good.

"Mr. Right" walked out of his house and got in the car. He must have really tried to dress to impress me. He looked and smelled amazing! I just smiled and said, "Well, I'm here!"

He said, "I didn't think you would really come."

To myself I was thinking, "Yeah, right." If only he knew I couldn't stop thinking about him the entire time! We went to the mall, then to eat, and enjoyed our time together. Marcy was excited that I was finally happy. I was thankful to have one true friend like her.

The night ended fast but didn't end without a kiss. We had already planned the next date. This time was completely different. I felt that it was really going to be serious. He was my knight in shining armor sent to rescue me. In that moment, I felt like a princess. With him I could conquer anything! He was my angel in disguise. God knew what he was doing when he sent this man.

Shaun and I continued visiting each other every week. We began rebuilding something that was unbreakable. We became focused and mature. He made it easy for me to leave all the mess behind me and start over. We went to senior prom together and began renting hotel rooms to spend time with each other. Our relationship was that of a modern-day Bonnie and Clyde without the crime! I didn't need anything or anyone but him. He was my strength through weakness.

CHAPTER 10
Leaving Home

May 2006, I graduated high school and received my diploma. A lot of people said I would never get that far. I was so thankful and appreciative that I did! Upon graduating I realized it was time for me to grow up and move on. I needed to experience life elsewhere. I couldn't continue living like I was or I would not make it. I began trying to find my purpose and understanding the things I went through. I learned that to do that, you must go through a process.

My parents sent me to a Job Corps place in Virginia. I took a Greyhound bus there, and I was only 17 at the time. It was an experience I can never forget. I had the best roommates and crazy experiences, and I learned a lot in my short time there. At the end of the day, I was taught to live on my own there and I changed a lot. However, before turning 18, I went back to Kentucky.

I missed Shaun and I thought there was more I needed to share with him. I wanted him to know the reason behind my negative, crazy ways that he had seen before. I really wanted to give him a part of me. The truth! He was a listening ear that didn't judge me. He wanted to help me in any way he could. He told me to come live with him. Of course we couldn't stay at his parents' house because they didn't believe in "shacking up." He told me not to worry, that he would make sure I was taken care of. I packed my things, and he came to pick me up.

My dad was mad that I was leaving. He didn't allow me to take my car that I paid for out of my weekly checks. It was in his name so there was nothing I could do about it. Shaun was upset when he saw what I dealt with at home. He didn't come from the type of family I did. There was a lot of confusion over time because we came from different backgrounds.

I was worried about stability, stressed about not knowing what to expect, and angry about my car. I wanted to be normal so badly but, for some reason, was impossible for me. I blamed myself for taking the hard road to deal with my mental issues. I resented my family for not being aware of what I went through, and I struggled with accepting who I really was. I was running away from what hurt me.

Our first night together, we had no place to go. Shaun had a key to his dad's church and we slept in his office. From there, we started looking for jobs. He found one first, but it was 30 minutes away. We had only one vehicle, so every day I had to ride to work with him, drop him off, and sit in the parking lot until his eight-hour shift was over. We didn't have gas money to ride around, and we didn't have friends or family to go see in the area. It was a struggle, but it had to be done.

A few weeks passed and he made friendships at work. It gave him the opportunity to catch a ride any time he needed. With that happening, I was able to get a job. We stayed at his friend's house and helped out in the meantime. We focused on getting our own place and settling down. Soon enough that happened for us.

Our first place we rented was in the projects. Rent was only $300 a month, so it was easy for us to come up with that amount to move in. We went to Goodwill and bought things we needed and found a couch up the street on the side of the road. We did what we had to do to survive. We learned to appreciate things a lot more.

Once his parents realized what was going on between us, they began offering help in any way they could. We rode to church with them every service, and they would take us to eat after services. We grew closer through their kindness and willingness to see we were OK. Over a period of time, we became inseparable. It was like they were meant to be my family! They were a part of my healing, acting like the parental figures I needed to overcome my unbalanced life.

Shaun and I would come home to our door standing wide open. We experienced a lot of crazy activities in our apartment complex. We steered clear of what was around us. We knew there was something better coming, so we held on for the ride. There were many times we both wanted to feel comfortable and live in a cleaner environment. We chose not to allow our wants to affect us.

My family didn't make my transition easy. My mom was the only one to call for the first few months, but she was always worrying. I had to stop allowing our conversations to get me upset. That's why I got away in the first place, because we clashed. Not just that reason alone but it was a big one. I quit answering her calls and everyone else's. I completely shut down emotionally and withdrew myself from them all. I battled something bigger than I was and wouldn't give up.

Shaun was very unselfish in his ways. He made sure I didn't go hungry and that I had my needs taken care of. In the four months we had lived together, I couldn't see myself with anyone else. He was truly my best friend and soul mate. I relied on him for everything and still didn't love myself enough to pursue my dreams. I just settled with getting by. One day at a time, my life was getting better.

In December 2007, he asked me to marry him. I said, "Yes!" We sat on the same couch that we got off the side of the road and laughed at everything we were going through. When he proposed there wasn't a ring. We couldn't afford a wedding, and I didn't expect any of that. We both knew all that mattered was being one, and the rest would work itself out.

My soon-to-be father-in-law, Bishop Elvis Baker, was an ordained minister. We spoke with him about marrying us. He prayed about it, and said, "God chose you two to be together!" He agreed to marry us. He suggested we receive marriage counseling in order to understand its importance. We agreed and that's when it all took place.

I was burdened by the fact that I probably would not have any family attend. Several of them didn't agree with interracial marriages at the time. They never admitted it, but they didn't have to. I was white and he was African–American. I wanted support from them, but I didn't at the same time. As a young girl, I always imagined a big wedding and all my family there. I didn't see it being that way in reality.

Dear Interracial Couple,

Don't worry about the looks and stares. If God has ordained your marriage, nothing will harm it. We have been called names and looked down on so many times. Likewise, we have been pierced with hurtful slander. I used to feel like I had to fight every battle. I caused a scene at many places because people would come against us. Oh, how I remember many times I let the enemy have his way with my mouth and actions. I speak against every weapon that is formed against your marriage. God, I ask you to transform the minds of people who fix their mouths against interracial families. God, I ask that you remove any hurt that anyone has felt from others who shamed them. Lord, I thank you for the refining of their perspective and renewing of their spirit. God, I praise you for the couples that have pushed through this hurt and continue to know that they are meant to last. We tear down the bondage of racism and replace it with undeniable love. We stand in unity as one! In the name of JESUS CHRIST, it shall be done! Amen.

Shaun and his dad had talked about the possibility of having a wedding ceremony at the church. I was unaware of their conversation at the time. He came home and told me, "Babe, my daddy is throwing us a wedding and there is nothing you need to do but invite who you want." I was so excited that this was really happening. We set the date for March 29, 2008. I was ready to be Mrs. Wilson!

I called and invited my family to attend. There were some hard words that came from a few. I had to ignore them and not let it hurt me. I knew what to expect in the first place. They didn't know what Shaun and I shared. I had nothing to explain to them, other than I wanted them to be there. I left the ball in their court whether or not they attended.

I forgot that I needed someone to walk me down the aisle. I asked myself over and over if I wanted my dad to have the honor. It was so hard deciding and emotionally draining. My dad was so sick, and we didn't know how long he had left. Doctors had given him up to five years left. His kidney disease, diabetes, and heart were really taking a toll on his physical abilities. I decided I wanted him to give me away, and I hoped it would change some things in our lives.

My aunt allowed me to take her 16-year-old wedding dress and have it altered to suit me. We had to get a big bow removed from the back and the puffy sleeves removed as well. Funny thing was, the dress was absolutely perfect for me! It had a gorgeous long train with all kinds of pearl and lace embellishments on it. By the time it was finished, it was absolutely beautiful.

We chose our wedding party and everyone bought their own dresses and suits. We could not have been more blessed with how everything was taking place. Our colors were yellow, black, and gold. Bishop did all of my floral arrangements and decorating the day before our wedding. I had not seen anything and didn't know what to expect until the day of. I didn't even know who would make it and who wouldn't. I just went with the flow of things.

We woke up the morning of our big day and got ourselves ready. Our wedding party was supposed to take us in separate cars to the church, but they forgot us. We ended up having to ride together. With all the last minute things needing to be done, we were a few minutes late arriving. It was embarrassing that we didn't make it on time, but we just giggled about it.

As we pulled into the parking lot, my eyes got large. I couldn't believe how packed it was. I was steadily looking to see if I recognized any of my family's vehicles. There were only a few that I could pick out. We ran into the church foyer and that's where the bridal party stood waiting to help us get together. The doors to the sanctuary were closed, so I couldn't see anything inside. My mom pulled me into the pastor's office and began talking to me about marriage. She was feeling me out to make sure I really wanted to go through with it.

After the big spew took place, my dad walked in crying. He held out his arm and said, "Are you ready?" I nodded my head and we locked arms. He briefly talked to me while the wedding party walked down the aisle. I couldn't believe we had even got to this point. I had so much bottled up emotion I couldn't talk. I had waited for this moment for years. I finally felt like a woman and I felt strength that I never had before.

The music began playing and the big doors swung open. I instantly began tearing up. The church was decorated so beautifully! I couldn't believe what Bishop had done all by himself. I looked around and there were more of my family members there than expected. The ones who showed were the ones who counted. Everything turned out perfectly.

Bishop went through our vows and gave a brief message to everyone there about interracial love. He gave a specific Scripture from the Bible about the Ethiopian woman's relationship; it was so powerful. You could hear people crying, and it was so quiet in the room that if a pin dropped it would have been noticed. His empowering speech shifted the atmosphere. There was purpose in our marriage. We said, "I do," and I became Mrs. Wilson.

After the service, a few of my family members came up to me, crying, and apologized to my husband. I was surprised that they really had a change of perception of our marriage. I knew God had a great deal in that happening. I thought that all I ever wanted was to hear them say, "I'm proud of you, and I accept you." It wasn't though. I soon realized there was more than that.

CHAPTER 11
My New Beginning

*B*eing married brought new obstacles and challenges. We had already lived together and knew we were going to be happy in that area of our life. There was more that we didn't realize beforehand though. We wanted babies, and I was told at the age of 15 there was a possibility I couldn't carry a child. I had an ovarian cyst and scar tissue that damaged me. It wasn't something that we really talked about until afterwards. It brought some doubt and sadness to even getting his hopes up. The thought of not being able to conceive made me feel like I couldn't do what a woman was made to do.

Shortly after getting married, we moved into a nice townhome in town. We had decent jobs and slowly made our home feel comfortable to our liking. People at church and friends around us asked the question every newlywed gets asked: "When are you going to have babies?"

We would always shrug it off and say, "When the Lord blesses us." It was no one's business when, so we didn't engage in details. We were just believing God for healing.

More things began surfacing throughout time. There were some things we hadn't told each other before. We both thought we knew everything about each other's life but we didn't. Being in Shaun's hometown, I found out about his previous relationships with people I knew through him. He found out about my secret life with Darren, which was before we got serious, but he was concerned. We both began resenting each other and growing jealous of one another. It was like all of a sudden our strong foundation was wobbly. We had betrayed our honesty and trust.

We started arguing over little stuff that didn't amount to anything. Eventually, we started drinking and smoking weed together. Then, we stopped communicating on the level we had before. We fell into the marital trap. Everyone looked up to us on the outside because our relationship appeared so strong. We didn't let outsiders see us any differently because we had fought so hard to get where we were. We just kept it closed up between us.

I would cry all the time about the smallest thing. Shaun was the complete opposite. He didn't show emotion. I realized we were two completely different people on that level. It was very hard to cope with the differences. He had always consoled me when I was weak, but our differences caused him to look at me differently. I had no one to talk to, and my world began spinning upside down again.

Shaun received a worship leader position in the city. We were excited for the new opportunity. He was so gifted in his talent, that I had faith it would take him far. The new church was a great setting, but it seemed the preacher wasn't there for all the right reasons. I'll go on to say, we weren't either. We were just babes in Christ. We were still learning how to grow. God allows us to go through valleys to strengthen us. Although this style was different, we wanted to embrace it. I believe, with an open mind and heart, you can get something out of anything.

Every Sunday we would attend service. The praise team was phenomenal and the congregation accepted us well. We were there for two months when I began getting sick. I noticed I had to go to the bathroom more than ever before, I was starving by the time service was over, and I stayed tired. All these changes were draining me. My sickness was a part of my blessing.

We had just rung in the New Year; 2009 was going to be our best. We set all kinds of resolutions for this year. A few were to lose weight, to grow in our marriage, and start a healthy lifestyle. I thought that I needed to eat less fast food and greasy stuff to feel better. It turned out it wasn't that at all. I took a pregnancy test, expecting yet another negative. Two bold lines appeared, and I couldn't believe what I was looking at. I was pregnant!

I ran out of the bathroom screaming and jumping. Shaun didn't know what was going on. "We are having a baby!!!" He had instant shock. Tears flowed down our faces, and we just wrapped our arms around each other.

I was not thinking clearly at that moment. My mind began racing a hundred miles an hour. I called the health department to see if I could get in immediately. I wanted a doctor to tell me this was really happening.

My appointment was set for a week later. The anticipation was real! I had no patience in waiting for results. I bought several more tests just to see if it were a false positive. It turned out all of them were positive, also. My heart was so full of joy; I was so thankful that God blessed me.

The day of my appointment, I went in and had my exam. Hearing the doctor say, "You ARE pregnant," brought so many emotions. She even told me my expected due date based on my last cycle. This was really happening. I wanted to start planning that day. I got set up with my ob–gyn, the same one who told me I possibly couldn't conceive years before. I was looking forward to seeing him.

We moved back to my hometown for support, and Shaun was working as a deputy jailor on third shift. He loved that line of work; he grew passionate about his position. I didn't like being home alone at night, but I dealt with it. I became obsessed with keeping healthy and taking my vitamins regularly. The pregnancy gave me a lot to look forward to. I would get on Pinterest and pin all kinds of stuff to my baby wall that I created. Pinning became my nightly routine.

Upon meeting with my ob–gyn, he was truly surprised that I was pregnant. He did an ultrasound of my stomach and let us hear the baby's heartbeat. He told me my pregnancy was helping dissolve the cyst. He said, "It happens like that sometimes because your body changes so much." Everything looked great and the baby was healthy. He set my due date for September 23, 2009.

I didn't know what to expect with becoming a mother. I never had another life to look out for other than my own. I had failed at so many things in my past years, but I vowed to be the best mom I could be. I knew there would be sacrifices that would come. All I focused on in the time being was having a healthy lifestyle and preparing for my baby's arrival.

Six months into my pregnancy, I grew close to my unborn child. I began seeing my belly stretch and feeling the flutters inside me. I was so in love already! The weeks following, I went in for an ultrasound to find out what our baby's sex would be. I was overwhelmed with excitement, just like other mothers. I waited with anticipation for my name to be called. Suddenly, the door opened and I walked back into the cold, dark room. "Are you ready?" the nurse asked. "Of course I am!" I giggled.

She began the ultrasound and Shaun was holding my hand as tightly as he could. He was just as impatient as I was. "It's a girl!!!" the nurse said. She flipped the lights on, and I began crying.

"Babe, you OK?" Shaun muttered.

"We are having a girl!!!" I yelled. As much as I wanted to dress her up, fix her hair, play dolls, and spoil her, I knew that I would have to protect her. I could never let her life be destroyed like mine was. So many thoughts and emotions hit me at once. All I could think about was the fact her papaw hurt me at one time. There was no way I could dismiss that thought. It began sinking in.

I couldn't sleep, and I wasn't able to focus on anything. My mind continually raced. What am I going to do? No one knows! My dad was sick, and I didn't want to be the cause of his death. He wasn't supposed to be stressed because his heart was so bad. I played out so many scenarios, asking myself question after question. I knew my mom would expect to keep her grandchild sooner or later. I just couldn't allow that to happen. It was up to me to keep her from being harmed.

Although I knew my dad wasn't the person he used to be, I wasn't about to take a chance. A month before my due date, I asked Mom if I could meet with her. She agreed and came to my house. Shaun said," I will stay by you, and don't stress." I knew it was something that had to be done. It was time to release the dark secret that I had hidden for 11 years. It was not going to be easy, but what in life is?

She sat down on the couch beside me. Her face showed concern. I began by telling her, "There was a reason for my addiction, sexual encounters, and attempted suicide." She looked confused and didn't know what I was about to say. That's when I told her the ugly truth.

She began cussing and went into a hysterical rage. "I knew it was something!! Why wouldn't you tell me?"

I told her, "The time wasn't right then but now it is." I let her know my baby couldn't stay all night with her and that if she wanted to spend time with her one of us had to be present. She was angry but very understanding.

After it processed, she was ready to snap on him. I begged her to not say a word. This was something I wanted to confront him about when the time was right. She thought about it and agreed to allow me to handle it with him. She left crying and very emotional. I knew that was going to change a lot in my family. I did feel some relief just talking to her about it, but I felt guilty for waiting so long. It was really bothering me and I couldn't shake it.

All over again, I was living in my past. My new beginning wasn't what I expected. The hurt, the anger, the disgusting details, and the pain returned. It was like someone pulled a trigger and the bullet shot through my heart. I had no control over my feelings. They persisted and didn't stop. My mind and heart were set on replay. There was no pause button. I realized in that time that I wasn't healed. I was running and swallowed up by my emotion. I needed help, and I was afraid of what I felt.

CHAPTER 12
The Gift of Life

*T*he miserable pain of the last days before giving birth was unbearable. I was more than ready to meet our princess. My mom and Shaun were by my side through all the Braxton Hicks labor and rushed me to the ER with every pain. It was nothing more than a part of pregnancy. I had my last doctor's appointment the day before my due date. I was hoping to go in and be told I was dilated enough to be admitted. Unfortunately, that wasn't the case. I was 2 centimeters, and the doc required me to be 3 centimeters. I was bummed, but what was one more day?

Shaun and I went to the local Walmart to pick up a few things. I power-walked the store, and after my second lap around, I went into labor. He rushed me to the hospital and that's when my water broke. It felt like I had peed on myself. I didn't even know that was the "water." They tested it, and sure enough it was almost time to have a baby. I was so nervous. I couldn't wait!!

I was determined to have our baby girl naturally. We finally agreed on a name. She was going to be born on the first day of fall, so we decided Autumn Grace was perfect. Now it was just time for me to get comfy and wait on her to make her grand entrance. The doctor came in, regularly checking my cervix. It was taking forever to dilate fully. I thought once your fluid breaks, it was immediately going to happen. Boy, was I wrong!

Fourteen hours later, I couldn't take the labor pains anymore and chose to get an epidural. It wasn't as bad as I expected or my pain was so bad I didn't care. My body went numb from the waist down and I couldn't feel anything. It was good and scary because I wondered if she was going to come out and me not know. That's when the doc came in for the last time.

My mother-in-law, who is a true woman of God, came and sat by my bed. She began praying and holding my hand. Shaun was on the other side of me and my mom was at the foot. I felt pressure, like I needed to push. The doc checked me and I was ready. Autumn was soon to arrive from the womb. I had my mind set and focused.

Upon pushing for two and half hours in five positions, yes, five positions, I had to be rushed in for an emergency C-section. She was stuck in the canal and my bones were too narrow for her to come through. I was so afraid but just wanted her to be OK. The doc rolled me into the room and began medication. It happened so quickly, that I didn't realize it was done. Out came my beautiful princess. I waited on her to cry and immediately she did.

Tears flowed down my face when I laid my eyes upon her. They took her out of the room and sewed me up. I wanted to hold her so badly but had to wait. I knew her daddy was waiting outside the door to see his angel. My heart felt a new love, something that I would have never imagined. It was a feeling of joy; I was so thankful. There is truly not a greater feeling than becoming a mommy.

I was admitted into a room and soon after they brought our baby in. I couldn't believe this beautiful gift God gave to me. She was absolutely perfect!! Dark hair, blue/gray eyes, long lashes, and beautiful skin. She weighed in at 7 pounds, 1 ounce and was born at 6:00 pm. I was so in love, and my mommy instincts became natural. I had no other worry in the world, other than her.

We stayed in the hospital three days, and I was recovering well from my surgery. I couldn't wait to get home and be comfortable in my own bed. I also couldn't wait to get our baby girl into her new home. We had decorated her room in purple and pink butterflies. She was set up for the arrival home. I felt badly that I couldn't move a lot, but her daddy went above and beyond to take extra care of our princess. I was thankful for his sincere love for our girl.

When we arrived home, Shaun and I just sat and stared at our baby. We were both lost in her eyes. She was everything and more than we imagined. Her favorite thing to do was eat, which was definitely a trait she got from us. Everything she did made us thank God even more. We were truly blessed with a healthy and beautiful child. Her life gave us life. She stole our hearts, and we couldn't imagine it any other way.

Months passed and we were used to not sleeping at night. We would rotate our schedules so that one could sleep while the other was on watch. It worked out great, but we didn't want to sleep because we loved holding her close to us. We managed to get by with as little rest as we could handle.

When Autumn was nine months old, we found out we were having another baby girl!!! My due date was March 24, 2011, five days before we celebrated our anniversary! She was a surprise to us, and we couldn't wait to have another angel to grow up with her big sister. God had blessed us, yet again. We knew we wanted to name her Trinity Faith. We chose Trinity because of its meaning: "the Father, Son, and Holy Spirit."

With this pregnancy, I had a lot of morning sickness and fatigue. I didn't have that with my first, so this was all new to me. It seemed to go by rather quickly. With this one, there was an automatic scheduled C-section for March 24, 2011. Boy was I glad that I wouldn't have to go through the pain of labor and pushing again. Once again, I practiced healthy eating and taking my vitamins. However, with her I craved McDonald's Big Macs. My husband went to McDonald's every morning as soon as lunch began and got me a Mac. I couldn't wait to eat it, and my mouth would water.

Overall, my nine months of pregnancy went smoothly. I guess a lot of it had to do with me knowing what to expect. We moved into a bigger house to have room for the arrival of our new princess. We talked to Autumn all the time about her new baby sister, and she loved to touch the stretch marks on my oversized belly. We decorated both of their rooms in butterflies and everything was pink/purple. We had everything prepared for the big day.

March 24, 2011 approached, and it was beautiful outside. Not hot and not cold, just perfect. I was scheduled to come in at 6:00 am to begin the procedure. As they wheeled me back to the surgery room, Trinity's godmother, Bethany, followed. She was such a spiritual role model in our life at the time. She never had any kids before, and she was widowed, a very prestigious and well-known lady in the community. We loved her so much because she loved us genuinely and was one of the best people you could meet.

Shaun stood outside the doors with my mom, his parents, and Autumn. Bethany stayed in the room and held my hand the entire time. She had never experienced anything like this, and she was so humbled to be a part of it. It felt nice to have her praying with me while my baby was coming into the world. Her soft, pure tone kept me calm. At that moment, I knew that she was meant to be in that room with me.

The doctor took more time getting her out than it took for Autumn. I could feel the tugs and pulls. Upon coming out she immediately began crying. She had a good set of pipes on her. Of course, I was emotional from all the excitement of my new baby girl. She weighed in at a healthy 7 pounds and 11.5 ounces. It was so amazing to see how much both of our girls looked alike except that Trinity was a replica of me and Autumn was a replica of her daddy. Yet there was so much resemblance in their features.

We now had two special gifts of life: two baby girls that we were responsible for giving an honest, happy, and true life. We knew that meant more than we were capable of providing on our own in this upside-down world. However, with God we knew all things are possible. Our children and our life were given to him. We grew a close relationship with our angels. Our goals were always to let them know we would protect them, live for God, and build a trust and love that they will always feel.

CHAPTER 13

It All Comes Tumbling Down

*P*ost-pregnancy I started getting depressed and dwelling on my emotions. It was hard for me to control my feelings. I was so happy but yet so stressed for no reason. It became a serious losing battle. My husband would always ask me, "What's wrong with you?" He didn't understand what I was going through. I understood that, but at the time I didn't want to hear it.

I started seeing a doctor because I was getting so sick. Every morning, I was waking up nauseated and having small sharp pains in my lower abdomen. The doctor would say, "You're overweight and that is an issue for stomach problems." I didn't buy it; I knew there was something else. No one should ever have to deal with it every single day. I stayed in a crabby mood and didn't care to go out of the house. I barely was able to do anything with my family.

I knew that I had to get the sickness under control somehow. It took two years of studying and testing my symptoms. In that time, I was diagnosed with PTSD, IBS, abnormal blood sugar, anxiety, and depression. I was only 24 years old and had been put on eight medications for daily use. They made me feel out of my head and lethargic. I tried taking them at different times of the day, but the way I felt was not normal. I was just so tired of not feeling good.

Nothing was going like it should. I wasn't able to find help any way I turned. I would even sit in church and pray to God for comfort. I felt like I was a 70-year-old woman. I became very jealous hearted when it came to my husband. The enemy attacked my mind so badly that I couldn't help but listen: "Why would my husband want me? All I do is complain about being sick! He's young and healthy. He can find better." That's just a few to name. I became over the top.

With him being a worship leader, he directed a praise team. There were more women than men. The women would call or text and ask information about different things. I sat and watched his expressions on his face, the laughter/excitement in his voice, and the focus he gave to them while answering their needs. I didn't want to be perceived as a jealous wife, so I let it bottle up inside of me. The anger I possessed began showing without me being able to stop it.

It got to a point that I'd question him. I'd get mad when he came home later than normal from practices, and I'd search his phone for any evidence I could find. When I couldn't find anything, I'd convince myself he was deleting stuff and hiding it well. It turned out that he was deleting stuff because he didn't want me to flip out over a female writing him, even if it wasn't intentional.

Our relationship grew sour. It became similar to how my parents functioned when I was a little girl. We would argue constantly, sleep in different rooms, and find it hard to spend quality time together. Neither of us would have ever imagined this happening, but it did. Also, our past was relived in every argument because that was our way of getting back at each other.

I was drowning in sorrow and fear. I didn't want to lose what I knew God created us to be. However, I refused to live in the situation we were in. I knew we both needed to grow up and quit getting mad over petty stuff, but it was easier said than done. I packed stuff for the girls and myself and left. We went to my parents' and stayed for a few days and then returned home. It took three times of me leaving to realize what I was doing to our babies in the process. Although they were young, I knew they could feel something was not right.

Once I realized what was happening, I vowed I wouldn't just up and leave again. It was time to be a woman and stand my ground and him to be a man and stand on his. Communication was the biggest part in finding this equal balance. It didn't solve all of our problems but it did help with the majority. I knew for me to get better, I had a long road ahead.

Financial stress and the battles that come with life were so overwhelming. We eventually moved back close to Shaun's parents for support with the kids if needed. We got good jobs that got us by and worked hard. Autumn began preschool, and I started taking college classes. Everything looked up from there, except for my health. I was still miserable with myself.

After a painful hospital trip from being completely doubled over, the doctor on duty ran some tests and recommended I see a gynecologist immediately. He didn't say what he thought it was but did mention further tests would need to take place. I was very scared of the look he had on his face. It was as if something may be very wrong.

I set up an appointment with the new ob–gyn. This man had been in practice for over 30 years. He had obviously seen more than the average doctor with his experience. I didn't want to underestimate him because of his age, so I went with it. That was one of the best decisions I had ever made.

He started with a normal routine pelvic exam. I was very sensitive in that area. Everything hurt as he pushed towards my cervix. He then explained to me it was very inflamed and that he wanted to do more tests, so he scheduled me for yet another exam where they would go in and do a LEEP procedure, which was burning cells off of my cervix to test them. It didn't sound appealing at all, and I was not looking forward to the pain it would cause. My choices had run out and this was my only option.

I returned for my next visit and they took me back to the surgery room. There were several machines I had not ever had used on me before. One was for electricity to go through this wand type of instrument. Others I wasn't sure about, but the electricity one had me freaked out from the get go. I dressed into my gown, took a deep breath, and meditated my mind for a minute. I mentally prepared myself for what was about to happen.

With no one by my side, I felt like I was facing this battle alone. I knew God obviously meant for it to be that way for a reason. I grew a little self-pity because of it. I wasn't going to run from what could make me better, but I wanted to. I wanted to walk right out the door and leave.

The doctor came in and talked to me briefly about the procedure. I lay back on the bed and that's when it started. The electricity wand lit up and when he put it inside me I jumped because of how tender I was. As the electricity flowed through my cervix, the smell of burnt flesh filled the air. It was gross and very painful. I kept trying to shut my feelings and mental aspect off, but I couldn't.

The procedure lasted over an hour. It was supposed to last only up to 30 minutes, but I had several places on my vaginal area that made it a longer process. As it continued, I thought to myself, "if it wasn't for my girls, I would rather die." It was one of the worst things anyone could feel. I knew if it ever had to be done again, I would refuse.

Once the doctor was finished, he showed me the cup full of these cells he retrieved from my cervix. It looked frightening, seeing it in a jar. He then proceeded to tell me, "I'm almost 99% sure this is cancer!" He didn't know to what extent and how bad, but he was sure it was possible. He asked me not to get upset or worry. We would get it taken care of, but it would take an average of four to six weeks in the lab to determine accurate results.

The worry and concern made me distraught the entire time. That was truly a long time to wait on serious results like these. I kept my phone by me at all times, waiting for the report. I went to work as normal and kept quiet until I found out whether it was cancer or not. I was totally beside myself, and it was very noticeable.

My phone rang a few days after my birthday, which was August 29, 2015. The doctor said it was confirmed: I had cervical/uterine cancer and I needed an emergency hysterectomy. I had so much faith that it wasn't going to be the C word that I became mad at God for not healing me. There was nothing I could do, and all I wanted was not to feel the pain, so we scheduled it a week away. That gave my husband and I time to let our jobs know and set up a plan.

Everything in that moment came tumbling down. I wanted to give up, but I knew I had to fight. My daughters could not be without a mother. My husband couldn't be left alone, and I myself had come too far to give up now. I refused to allow myself to fail! If I could overcome addiction, I was able to overcome this illness. I had to encourage myself; no one else could do it for me. My prayer life became more than ever before.

CHAPTER 14

Discovery and Forgiveness

I went to church and prayed for the Lord to help me and bring me out of the surgery. As much as I wanted to be better, fear of everything that could go wrong set in. I had already previously had two C-sections and didn't like the thought of being opened up again. The church service that night was very liberating. I could feel Gods presence, in a powerful way. I knew he was going to do something.

A lady came to me and began praying. Without her knowing anything regarding my past or current well-being, she prophesied over me. She said that a generational curse was put upon my family, and the curse would stop with me. In that moment I wasn't sure what she meant. I began to feel a fire flow from my hands. It was a tingling, burning sensation that was definitely God working on me. She continued to say, "God has given you a gift of healing." I felt it take place. It was indescribable, but I found a peace in that moment.

A couple of days after that church service, my mom and aunt came to my house. I hadn't seen my aunt in a long time. We talked about all kinds of stuff about life. We went out to take a ride and our conversation became heavy. I found out that I wasn't the only one who carried dark secrets. They both had their own that, unfortunately, never came out until now.

My aunt didn't know about my molestation until that day. She cried and told me the true reason she never came around the family was because she and her other sister were raped repeatedly by a relative. My mom was angry she told me and became upset. I couldn't believe that I was never told anything about this occurrence. The person who did it had just passed a few years before, and my aunt was sitting by his bedside when it happened. He asked while on his deathbed that she be contacted. That was why!! He knew that he had to make it right with her. Come to find out, that was exactly what happened.

The sadness behind the undeniable truth was intense! It all made sense. The generational curse, the family problems, the anger, violence, and addictions. All of it became very clear to me. I began seeing things in a different matter after hearing her story. The deepness of forgiving but not forgetting was powerful. I began thinking about what continued to control my mind. If I truly find forgiveness, I will break the curse! It wasn't long after that I had a bad dream that my dad was on his deathbed and couldn't speak. I saw myself holding his hand saying," I forgive you!" not knowing if he really heard me. I woke up out of my dream crying and vowed that I wouldn't let it happen like that.

A few weeks prior to surgery, I called my dad and told him I was coming to visit and that I needed to talk to him. He was so weak that he was barely able to hold a conversation on the phone. I wanted finally to break free of the shackles I was bound by. I wanted to make things right before my surgery. If something were to happen, I would never get the chance to do it again. I knew it was now or never.

My husband, our girls, and I went for a visit. When the time was right and no one was in the room, I engaged in conversation. My palms were sweaty and my heart was racing. I almost couldn't do it, but I built up the courage somehow. I looked him in the eye and told him my feelings.

Dad was silent. He acted as if he couldn't believe I knew this entire time. I explained to him that what happened has haunted me all these years and I wanted an apology and closure on what took my life and ripped it apart. He cried and looked out into the field in front of the house. He shook his head and couldn't speak at first.

The dead silence was excruciating. Even more, he began denying remembrance of what I was talking about. I lashed back every time he tried to deny it. "You know what you did!!! I'm giving you one chance to make it right! You're on your deathbed, for Christ's sake, isn't that enough?"

He sobbed and continued with, "I don't remember, but if I did, I am sorry!" What was I really expecting? I was so upset that it was coming to this. All I wanted was for it to be over!!!!

We left their house and took the long, quiet road back home. My husband tried consoling me, but all I did was cry. I was so angry that it didn't turn out the way I wanted. I just wanted him to say, "I'm sorry," and acknowledge his wrongdoings. Enough time had passed that I figured he would make it right. Our daughters loved their papaw, and he truly stepped up to be there for them. Although they weren't ever around him alone, he played with them more than anyone. I knew everything had changed in him except forgiveness.

I didn't linger too much on my hurt feelings. I had to focus on my upcoming surgery and spend time with my family while I could. A week later my phone rang. "Tabby?" my dad said from the other end.

"Yeah, Dad, it's me."

"I'm sorry!" he cried aloud. A sudden silence and heartbreak filled the phone line. I couldn't speak, and I couldn't see from the heavy tears.

I finally replied, "Sorry for what?"

"You know what! I was wrong and I'm sorry. Can we just leave this behind us and start over?" he said.

"I wouldn't want anything more than that," I shakily replied. It was over! Done! The guilt, hurt, shame, and defeat were leaving my soul. I felt like I was being cleansed! Peace was raining over me. I was ready to start a new life and be done with the past. No more looking back from here. I was given a fresh start to find my happiness again. Through the discovery of my family's secrets, I found peace in mine. It was a day I'd never forget as long as I live.

The day before my surgery, I went back to spend time with my parents. It was awkward and peaceful at the same time. Dad was very sick but managed to take the girls on a ride in his power chair. He took them for a stroll around the block to show all his neighbors his grandbabies. We laughed and enjoyed every minute of the quality time we were given. No more flinching when he would rub my shoulder. No angry backlashes when he would joke, and no tension was left in our home. It was God's peace that surrounded us.

CHAPTER 15
Going under the Knife

September 12, 2015 I went in to prep for my surgery at around 7:00 am. It seemed like I waited forever before they took me back. Shaun and my mother were by my side. They waited outside the doors, when I got on the operation table. "Tabatha count with me as I put this mask on you," the doctor said.

"5, 4, 3, 2, 1." I was out!

"Huhhhuhhhhhh," I gasped for breath. I woke up to severe pain and numbness, along with low oxygen. I couldn't breathe! I began to panic and nurses swarmed me to help.

"Tabatha we need you to breathe slowly. Deep breaths in and out, Honey. Don't panic. You're going to be OK. Turn the oxygen to 5," one nurse hollered. "Raise the bed slightly," another nurse said. I stared at the ceiling, trying to regain control of my breathing.

Slowly, I was feeling air in my lungs. It was hard to breathe, but I was maintaining it. "My husband! Please, my husband!"

"Sweetheart we will get him. First we have to make sure you are OK," the nurse countered. I shook my head. "Are you in pain?" she asked. Again, I nodded. She sent someone to get pain medication to put in my IV. When they returned, she injected it and I drifted away again.

Upon waking up, I felt my breathing was more controlled but still weak. I looked over and my husband was by my side. I felt relief in that moment. This pain I felt though was intense and very sharp. The pain medicine wasn't helping me at all. They came in every hour and kept giving it to me. It lasted for maybe 20 minutes each time. I knew that something was wrong. I kept telling them that this was in no way normal.

After hours of crying and complaining, my doctor came in. He said I would be in pain for a while. They had to do some extra stuff while inside of me. My bladder had fallen, and they had to tack it up as well. I couldn't handle it though. I just wanted answers. At this point, I began praying that God relieve this pain. I felt hopeless and miserable!

Two days later, nothing had changed. My breathing had gotten better, but the rest didn't. The doctor surprisingly released me to go home. I knew I wasn't ready, but it was his order. My husband and baby girls were there, waiting on me. My girls said they would take care of me with their Doc McStuffins kits. The love and caring of their little hearts made me forget what I felt.

Upon getting home, nothing made me comfortable. I didn't want my kids to see me crying and hurting the way I was. As much as I tried to hide it, I just couldn't. It was so bad that I told God I'd rather die than to feel the pain. Those were serious words to speak, considering what I was going through. I didn't really want to give up. I had two angels to take care of. However, that goes to tell you just how bad it really was.

I didn't sleep at all the first night. I just babbled about what I was going through. My husband said, "I am taking you back to the hospital. They have to do something." We got back in the car and drove back to the hospital. They immediately took me back. After running some tests, they called the doctor in.

Apparently, when they tacked my bladder up it was sewn into a nerve. The doctor gave me two choices: (1) I could be opened back up, or (2) he could give me stronger medication. He gave me a stomach massage to help detach the stitches from the nerve. I was not about to go through being opened up again, twice in two days. That was just out of the question. Then I didn't want to take stronger meds due to being afraid of becoming addicted again. It was a tough decision to make.

After a lot of thought, I decided to take the medication and do the massage on my belly. I was so sore that it made it worse, but I knew in a few weeks I'd be glad I did. I had my husband control my medication. I didn't take the strong pain killer unless it was an absolute have to, which turned out happening once a day for a few days. The massaging wasn't helping much. I thought this was going to be a lifelong battle.

Through the trouble, I found myself once again seeking God. I prayed so hard and cried so much that I knew he must have heard me. I asked for healing and strength. I knew through him, "All things are possible." He had delivered me from so much before. Why couldn't he do so this time? Although my prayers weren't being answered when I wanted them to be, I still believed.

My faith grew stronger in my weakness. My heart grew humbler in my valley, and my mind was constantly focused on prayer. I realized it was meant for me to go through this. At the time I didn't know why. I was a little angry. However, God's purpose is never to question.

After a week of suffering, I woke up out of my sleep. I had to use the restroom and felt a complete difference in my body. I began moving around, feeling my stomach, and stretching to see if the pain was still there. With a confused look on my face, I glanced in the mirror and raised my shirt in disbelief. I was healed!! God had once again showed up. I was so thankful, I began to laugh, cry, and lift my hands to worship. Many times I had failed him, yet he never failed me.

It took approximately four weeks to recover fully and get out of the house. I felt better than I had in a long time. No more waking up sick to my stomach, no sharp pains, and no more sleepiness throughout the day. I truly felt that I had been given a new body. Two years of sickness were gone, just like that. I continued to read God's word and pray, for I knew his purpose was going to be great.

Through my healing process, God showed me that this was meant to be a part of my testimony. Sometimes, it takes enduring something we cannot control to get our attention. In the moment of suffering, you gain many emotions, doubts, and fears. I learned that through those emotions, you also gain vision. God has to put us in a place of weakness, so he can strengthen us. I went to a new level in my spiritual life. I learned to praise him in the good and the bad.

CHAPTER 16

Death at Every Corner

Shortly after celebrating my baby girl's sixth birthday, tragedy began taking place. It was on a cold October day that I received a call that an old friend, Sam, had been found dead. She was found in a rundown hotel room, overdosed from drugs. I couldn't believe it was really her. She has a smile that lit up any room, and a heart that was so pure. I didn't even know she was addicted. Sam was really family to me. We were all very close but lost connection over time. Her husband was very abusive and controlling over her, not allowing any of her friends or family to associate.

An autopsy had to be done before they would release her for a funeral. I wanted to help the family any way I could with finances, so I used social media to reach out. She had left behind three beautiful little boys that were ages 7 months, 3 years, and 5 years old. They had to be placed in a relative's home after the fact due to her husband's arrest as a suspect for her death and other previous warrants. He was known for his drug habits and without a doubt led her down the same path.

It was horrifying to say the least. A group of us girls who grew up together attended her funeral. She didn't look anything like we remembered. She was skin and bones, very pale, and obviously sick before her passing. You could see scars from her picking her face beneath the makeup. It was hard to see her at the young age of 26 lying there dead.

I began thinking of how that could be me. How far God had brought me. It was painful to stand over her casket and know that the enemy took out such a beautiful soul. I said a few words and mourned to myself. I didn't want to question God, but in that moment I truly didn't understand why something so bad happened to someone so good. It took a long time for the toxicology reports to return. When they did, it showed that she died from toxic cocaine and methadone overdose.

A few days after her burial, we received another disturbing call, one that we never saw coming. My husband's granny went into a coma. They called us to the hospital, and we immediately rushed to her side. She was the granny that we lived by for a long time. She kept us on the straight and narrow. She genuinely loved us both, and my husband loved her even more. She was the only biological grandmother he had left, and she was his heart.

He was broken to hear that she was on life support. We sat by her bedside with hope that she would just wake up. Unfortunately, that didn't happen. She became an angel, and we were truly hurt that we loss such a special influence in our life. My husband went through so much that I knew I had to remain supportive for him. He needed me more in that moment than ever before.

We would always call Granny late at night and talk about everything you could imagine. She was a night owl and not your average grandmother. Her personality was one of a kind. She loved to dress nicely and match everything to the tee. She was truly special and would be missed a lot. We spent time with the family and attended the arrangements that were being made. It was so hard to process; reality just wasn't kicking in.

The day of her viewing, we walked in and my husband broke. He stayed at her casket for a while, asking God why. Two deaths just a few days apart made me numb. I didn't know how to feel. I just stayed strong on the outside. Our daughters were upset, and I allowed them to express their feelings. I hated that they had to lose their granny so young. She loved them very much.

We laid her to rest and tried to get back into a normal lifestyle. It was still hard to cope, but we knew life must go on. We both went back to work and began getting in the routine of normalcy again. We tried to remain focused on what Granny would have wanted if she were still here. She definitely wouldn't want us to stop our life and lose control of what was important, so we continued moving forward.

On my days off work, I went to visit my parents as much as I possibly could. The girls loved going to see their papaw and riding on his scooter around the block with him. I was enjoying the relationship we were building. It was nice to feel like there was nothing to hide and nothing to fear.

My dad celebrated his 51st birthday on November 24, 2015. I wasn't able to attend because I had to work. Mom told me he was very sick and had a lot of fluid on him so he was not really in the birthday spirit anyway. That was something very normal for him. He had dialysis that morning and still retained excessive fluid on his body. There were times the fluid was so bad that it would seep out of sores on his legs. The suffering he endured was unheard of.

Four days after his birthday, my husband and oldest daughter were out of town. Our youngest girl Trinity and I were home. We fell asleep on the couch, and my phone rang. It was 2 am exactly. No one ever called that late at night. I looked at the caller ID and it was my mom. Screaming and crying she told me I needed to get to the hospital now. "They are bagging your daddy, Tabby. It doesn't look good." This had happened many times before, but without thought I grabbed my baby and the keys and flew to the hospital.

The hospital was an hour and a half away. It was pouring rain and black as ever outside. In my heart, I felt something wasn't right. It's like I could sense death. I began praying, "God please don't take my daddy!! Please Lord! We've lost enough people. Don't take him." I began crying and my heart was aching. I could hear my dad's voice speaking to me. "Slow down. You have that baby with you. Slow down!" His voice was so clear.

It took forever to get there, being that it was raining so badly. My phone kept ringing. Different people were calling and checking on us. I just knew something was wrong. I could hear it in everyone's voice. I begged them for updates on what was going on all the way there. No one said anything, other than "They're working with him."

I pulled up to the hospital and some family met me at my car. They grabbed Trinity and stood outside. My mom was nowhere in sight, so I ran in. I could hear loud cries as I walked through the hallways. I didn't have to ask for his room; I followed the noise. I walked in with expectation of hope, yet it was too late.

There were no doctors working on him, no machines buzzing, and no oxygen connected to his nose. There was a tube sticking out of his mouth with nothing connected to it. I began screaming in disbelief. I grabbed his hands and they were already cold. I rubbed his hair, cleaned his face, and lost myself in the moment. Mom sat and cried without saying a word!! "Why? Why? Why? God, why?" I screamed in anger.

"Tab, calm down. I know it hurts, Baby," my mom muttered.

"No you don't! No one knows what this feels like!" I said foolishly. I felt like I was having déjà vu. I had envisioned this moment before. My heart was shattered and ripped apart. I could literally feel the brokenness. It was deeper than ever before. I had hoped that God would heal him and let us continue to bond as father and daughter again. Everything that I experienced in that moment was what I had dreamed months before. Had I not made it right with him when I did, I may not have had the chance.

The coroner came in and briefly gave his condolences. I didn't want to release my daddy's hand. I wanted to hold it forever. They rolled him out the door and loaded him in the back of the hearse. I needed my husband so badly, but he was hours and many miles away. I couldn't even think straight. I was completely beside myself.

My aunt drove my car to my parents' house, and I rode with some family. Shaun had called and said he was on his way. I walked into the house and ran to Daddy's room. The shoes he always wore lay in the floor, his oxygen monitor on the side table, and his oxygen machine where it had always been. Everything was in its place as if he were there. I lay in his bed and cried in agony. "This is all a dream!" I kept telling myself.

Unfortunately, the more I looked around, the more I realized it was reality. My dad was really gone. I didn't close my eyes all night. The sun came up and everyone started coming to the house before we went to make his arrangements. I didn't want to talk or be around people.

I was grieving harder than I ever had before. Shaun had finally made it, and he grabbed me, crying. Even that didn't heal my heart. I was so glad to have him there, but I was so broken that I couldn't relieve my mind from the pain.

I went to make arrangements with my mom and brother. We had to choose a poem for his obituary. My mom let my brother and I do the honor. We went through over a hundred, but there was only one that we thought was perfect. It reads as follows:

A million times we've needed you,
A million times we've cried.
If love alone could have saved you,
You never would have died.
In life we loved you dearly,
In death we love you still.
In our hearts you hold a place
No one else will ever fill.
It broke our hearts to lose you,
But you didn't go alone.
Part of us went with you,
The day God took you home.

The poem was exactly what we felt. It made us cry even more. We just finished up and went back home.

People brought food and cards. I didn't recognize half of them. I was physically in my body but mentally somewhere else. I randomly busted out with screams and hurt. I went through so many levels of emotion that I thought I was going to have a nervous breakdown. Nothing anyone did helped. I was a mess.

The next day, Tuesday, December 1, 2015 was my dad's visitation at 1:00 pm. I got dressed and slowly moved around the house. I hadn't eaten, and I was very sick. My eyes were swollen from the uncontrollable tears. The family went to the funeral home first. Our girls had just watched their granny being buried, and we didn't want them to see their papaw, also. So I had Shaun walk them in to view him first, and my aunt took them back to the house after.

As I walked down the long aisle, looking at the casket before me, I was torn. They decorated the funeral home in the most beautiful angels that lit up. He was surrounded by angels. His casket spray was one of the most beautiful pieces I ever laid eyes on. It had blue flowers and had a glass stairway to heaven piece in the middle of it, with a tall glass angel that glistened from a distance.

Not prepared for this moment, I completely shut down. I looked over at his casket and there he lay. He looked healthier in death than he did in life. All the fluid was gone, and he looked like the dad I had as a little girl. I stood there staring at him. I grabbed his hand and kissed his forehead. I cried so much that my eyes became dry. I sat in the wingback chair beside him and refused to move. As everyone came in they spoke and proceeded to hug me. I couldn't say anything; I would just nod.

A man walked up and handed me an envelope. This man was someone my dad knew when I was just a little girl. I recognized him but wasn't sure who he was at first. He said, "You may not remember me. I was a close friend from Domino's. Your daddy asked me to give you this before he passed. I'm sorry this happened, but he loved you very much and he wanted you to know that." The knot was back in my throat and I hugged the man, crying.

I sat down and looked over at Daddy in the casket. I opened the envelope, and it contained pictures of my dad and his Domino's crew at an amusement park. Right after I was born, he had taken this trip and won me teddy bears from the games he played. There was one picture in specific that shattered me. My dad was holding a Scooby Doo dog that he gave me when I was three years old. I carried it everywhere I went and never put it down. Receiving these pictures from him was like receiving them from Dad himself.

After it was over, we went to his mom's house, my favorite granny's. She was so depressed that I wasn't going to bring her down more with my sadness. I wanted to be there for her, like she always had been for me. We picked at a few bites of food and talked about all the good memories of Dad: his silly comical jokes, his laugh, his picking at people, and his favorite sayings. I realized how much I missed all of the good stuff before the bad started. I just wanted to say so much to him and couldn't. It was truly hard to deal with.

The next day was his funeral, and Shaun played and sang for it. It was nothing short of a peaceful homegoing. They loaded his casket in the hearse and we followed behind. I looked at the all-white Cadillac in front of us the entire ride to the cemetery. It was sinking in that he was about to be buried six feet under. Not only was that hard, but he was being buried beside my baby brother who had passed when I was three years old.

We arrived at the cemetery and said our final goodbyes. As I walked away, a piece of my heart went with him. There was no turning back to get a hug or hold his hand. It was over and done. All that I had left were his memories. I chose to remember the good and leave the bad. He was saved and made it home. God gave us both the privilege of a second chance.

CHAPTER 17
Family Broken

When death happens so close to home, it can either make you or break you. For my family, everyone was unfortunately left broken. My granny mourned daily and lost the happiness she once had. My mom was lost and confused; she felt that she had the weight of the world on her shoulders. My 16-year-old brother chose not to express his feelings openly. Therefore, he just remained silent and stayed in his room day and night. I knew deep down he must be torn just as we all were. As for me, I felt that I was given the one thing I waited for all my life and it was taken from me too quickly.

My mom was withered and overworked, swallowed up by her anger and hurt!! She tried to overcome her emotions by staying busy. She stayed overnight at a friend's house and ran the roads every weekend. This was not normal for her, and I could tell that she needed help. I would get random phone calls from relatives telling me she was a completely different person. I knew she needed me and needed time to heal. My momma was broken, lost, and confused. This is where I wanted to step up and do my part.

My husband and I decided to move in with her and help relieve some burden. I wanted to be there for my brother and give her room to find herself. All of her life she only knew this man and lived under his control. I vowed never to move back to that town for as long as I lived. I guess you shouldn't ever say, "Never!" We packed up and moved into my parents' doublewide. We had intentions of only staying a short period of time, and we lasted for about five and half months.

While Mom was battling the darkness of her anxiety and hurt, she struggled with finding her place as a widow. She would come home after work, stay on her phone, get a shower, and go to her friend's every day. There were times she would tell me, "Tab, feed your brother and make sure he doesn't need anything." Then she would walk out the door and not return until late in the morning. She was tormented by the pain, and as long as she was busy, she was fine. However, every time she came home, she was reminded of that dark emptiness.

I grew frustrated with the situation and didn't understand why it was so hard for her to get a grip on life. I would always talk about counseling, therapy, or resources for her to seek! She would respond, "I am a grown woman and there isn't anyone going to tell me what to do with my life." From there, I stepped back and realized only God knew what she needed. Our relationship had friction, and I was hurting more than helping. I get it though. She was my mom, and she didn't want my advice.

Tension grew thick in our house. In these few months, I can count the times she spent with us. I was tired of the noncommunication and disconnection I felt between us. This was something I couldn't get past because she took care of anyone else who would call. She hated this house and she would leave if it weren't for my brother. I knew that. That was her reason for blocking out all the things that were really important in her life. I understood on some level, but I didn't agree with how she threw us to the side like we weren't important.

A few months into us living at my parents', I found out my mom had moved on in another relationship. She began seeing a friend of my dad's, and I was angry. Technically, this guy had befriended her first, but still I was mad. He was much older than she and had previously lost his wife. My dad had said months before he passed that he thought Mom was cheating on him with this man. We would make jokes at Dad and say, "He's crazy. Mom isn't that type of woman." So when I found out she was seeing this guy, it made me think Dad was right all along. In reality, she never did, and I know that now. However, at the time, I wanted nothing to do with her or him.

I grew hard feelings because I thought Dad hadn't been gone long enough for her to move on already. She stayed at his house every night, and I was bothered that she was creating a completely different life that didn't involve us. Although, we wouldn't have wanted to be a part of it, I felt if he loved her, he would show it better by making an effort to get to know us. Mom had nothing but good things to say about him, and she would shut down anything negative I said. I felt like she was making a mistake and was worried that she was just moving on to feel wanted again.

Nothing was like it used to be before my dad's passing. We never had a completely stable household, but we did eat together around the table, watch movies, show love, and bond. It was evident that all of that changed when Dad passed. There was a change in our family's relationship. My dad's side of the family was close with my mom, and I assume she felt different while she was trying to move on. All the while, her side of the family never liked my dad anyway and was glad to see her happy with someone else.

What used to matter didn't matter any more. In my perspective, Dad was the glue that held us all together, and I didn't realize it until he was gone. My younger brother and my granny became my only concern. I couldn't dwell on what was going on or I knew it would swallow me up, just as it had everyone else. I would entertain the drama for a while because I couldn't control my feelings. Once I had a reality check, all that changed. I gained vision and clarity. God began healing my brokenness and transforming my mind. I slowly began overcoming the hurt and healing in the process.

Dear Mom,

I want you to know that I love you, and I am sorry for all that I put you through. You are the one person that I can count on, anytime that I need. I know that our relationship wasn't strong, and I did a lot that hurt you. I pray that you will forgive me and that someday we will be stronger than we ever have been. I forgive you and thank you for all that you have done. When I began writing this book, I wrote from a place of anger and hurt. Over the years, I went back and revised it so many times. I see how God has allowed me to see things through your eyes, and I now know that I was not easy to get along with. If I had the opportunity to go back, I wouldn't have changed a thing because I have grown from all of this. I do not ever want you to feel like you did something wrong, because you didn't. There was a purpose for everything that happened. I pray that God blesses you beyond your imagination. I pray that he heals your pain, and I pray that you see your value in him. Mom you have a purpose. You are genuine and care for people on a level that many don't understand. I have watched you give even when you didn't have and be strong even when you were weak. You would give gifts on Christmas, birthdays, and every other holiday. Then receive nothing in return. This was a burden that I carried for you, and you didn't even know it. I know that had to hurt you, along with all of the other things. This will be no more!!! I am speaking over our relationship and your life! YOU ARE SOMEBODY AMAZING. YOU ARE VALUED. YOU ARE LOVED. WHAT YOU HAVE BEEN THROUGH DOES NOT DEFINE YOU. THE ENEMY CANNOT HAVE YOU. YOU ARE SET FREE FROM ALL OF THE GUILT, HURT, SHAME, AND DEFEAT!! THE ANXIETY WILL LEAVE RIGHT NOW AND NOT RETURN. YOU WILL HAVE CLARITY LIKE NEVER BEFORE. YOU WILL NOT HAVE TO DEPEND ON ANYONE ELSE FOR ANYTHING, AND YOU WILL LIVE YOUR BEST LIFE STARTING TODAY!! IN JESUS' NAME!! AMEN!

CHAPTER 18
The Impossible

*L*iving in unhappiness and feeling as if you have no purpose will cause anyone to grow weary. I did not want my husband and children to suffer from the unethical reasoning for our being there. We had a family of our own and we needed to focus on us instead of on everyone else. That's when I began to pray a new prayer and receiving provision for what God was doing.

I asked God, "Lead us where you would have us to be." I believed that he had more for my family than my small town gas station job, struggling to make ends meet, and fighting battles that weren't ours to fight. I would read encouraging Scriptures in my Bible and truly seek him for help. I had an urgency for change, and I was ready to move forward in life. I didn't know how I was going to do it, but I found that the Bible held my answers. I had to learn how to pray and build a true relationship with Christ. Every time I secretly and humbly went before the Lord, I would open my Bible, and he gave me clarity on the Scriptures. I cannot tell you how amazing it was to get a word every time I looked. He never failed me and showed me that he had been there the entire time. It was a matter of me seeking him for the answers and not trying to do it on my own.

As I grew stronger in wanting to find my purpose, I could see his glory in all things, feel his presence in the room, and hear his voice speak to my heart. My faith and trust were in him and not in myself. The Scripture says, "We can do all things through Christ, who strengthens us." Without a doubt I knew that was the solution to everything that hurt me, hunted me, controlled me, and used me. In order to stop the chain reaction of pain, I must give it to him and change my way of thinking. God is waiting for us to lean on him and not our own understanding. He is the way, the truth, and the life!

One night, my husband and I were sitting up watching TV. We struck up a conversation about how we were tired of the life we were living. It was like God spoke loud and clear to get on indeed.com (a job search site that I got on a lot). I went to the site and God guided my steps to search for "contemporary worship leader needed." I thought to myself, "OK, why am I even doing this?"

I told my husband and with little enthusiasm, he said, "Yeah, let me know what you find."

Nothing had come up in our area, and right before putting my phone down I was led to search in the entire United States. I thought it was wishful thinking and crazy myself. I couldn't imagine leaving the state of Kentucky behind me. Although, I wanted to many times, I never saw it really happening. I continued to search anyways. I was "outside the box" of my normal.

There were over a hundred churches looking for someone all over the United States. I had nothing more to do, so I started going through their requirements and background. I looked at each one to see if anything connected with my family. There was one that I couldn't get past. Every time I scrolled away to look for others, I was drawn back to it. I didn't know what it was about this one church. I just felt that gut feeling!

The qualifications that the church listed were a degree, accountability, contemporary worship style, and ability to read music. Those were just a few of many. I was discouraged because my husband was so amazingly anointed but did not have a degree. On the contrary, he also did not read music. I told him this undeniable feeling I had and told him we should look it up to see if there was a webpage or Facebook page.

We began our search and found the church's webpage. Immediately it looked like our kind of place. It was very diverse, which was what we wanted as a diverse couple. The people looked very involved and the organization of the church's services was a plus. I focused to see more and find out why I was so drawn to this particular place.

I went far enough to find the pastor and first lady on Facebook. My motivation encouraged me to reach out and inquire about the position that was posted. Without my husband knowing that I reached out, seeking the position, I waited eagerly for a reply. Within just a couple of days, my answer came.

The bishop/pastor of this church, located eight hours away in the state of Michigan, sent back a very powerful and real comment. He asked why I was the one reaching out on behalf of my husband and not him. At first I was appalled. Then, I continued reading his sincere and modest statement. He said he wanted someone on his team who wanted it for themselves and could be a strong leader. He followed by saying, "Please have him to contact me on behalf of his interest." I respected his way of handling business with order and excellence.

I didn't want to say, "Well, sir, my husband has no clue. I got overly excited and randomly decided to write you on his behalf." So I just got angry at my husband for not taking the initiative to do it himself. I felt he was a procrastinator in "stepping outside his box." I started an argument for that silly reason before our day even got started. The spit spat was so heavy, he chose to leave and cool off at some family's house for a few days. Something so small blew up into a huge situation.

With him leaving, it made us both question our marriage. I was fed up with the repeat actions on both of our behalf. All I wanted was change in our focus. I realized I was pushing too much at once, but I wanted to see us both better our family life. Everyone is different in how they handle things, and he and I did not look at life from the same perspective.

Three days after, when Shaun returned home, we sat down and discussed our feelings with each other. He understood why I wanted him to take a fresh step into the unfamiliar aspects of change while I understood his opinion of why I should not be so pushy just because I see things differently from him. We were two different people who balanced each other out in a positive way. It was a matter of keeping it positive and not allowing it to have a negative impact on our marriage.

Immediately, with understanding, Shaun began researching the church for himself. He started conversing back and forth with the pastor and leaders of the church. We started having conference calls, followed by driving to Michigan and attending service for ourselves. Our experiences were something we felt had been missing a long time. The atmosphere and realness of the church and congregation brought happiness and hope in our life.

After many conversations, the pastor stated, "there was never an ad put up on indeed for their church." I felt a little crazy when he told us that. I didn't want them to think this was some kind of hoax, so I began searching it again to prove that it was on there. Sure enough, it was not found. There was no evidence of how this amazing opportunity came about, other than it was just God.

We drove the eight hours back to Kentucky, feeling better than we did going to Michigan. We didn't want to jump into anything until we had confirmation that this was for a purpose. Many of those arose, from a "How to get to heaven from Michigan" pamphlet that I randomly found on my register at work to continued conversations with the new friends we gained. It was without a doubt meant for us to relocate. We then began looking for a home and getting packed up.

CHAPTER 19

Pure Michigan

*T*ime went by fast, and we found the perfect house for our family. We ran into a few struggles before our moving day. Our car blew up, money was low, and we weren't sure how we were going to make it there. With all this happening, my family voiced their opinions, saying this was a sign that we better not do it. However, I knew nothing that is good will come easy. If God brought us to it, he will bring us through it.

Normally in situations that I had no control of, I would panic and back out. With this one, I felt a will to fight and push through. I wanted a new life, a new start, and peace. My husband and I were already married for eight years. At this point, it was time to spread our wings and fly. I was not allowing my focus to be sidetracked.

I booked the U-Haul to be picked up in the town in which we lived. With no transportation to bring with us and no one to follow behind us, I knew I needed to find something with a large cab to fit our family of four plus our small dog, Lucky, whom we could not leave behind. I knew this was going to be a challenge, but I was not giving up. I was proud of the strong mind-set that was instilled in me. I knew it was God's will. Some called it "plain crazy."

July 25, 2016 was the day we planned to make the journey to Michigan. On that day, my mom took me to pick up the U-Haul. The place I was scheduled to pick it up didn't have it. The nearest place that had my size truck was 35 minutes away and was in the middle of no-where. My mom, being the over-stressor she is, was mad that we had to go that far to get it. She made comments and sighs all the way there about, "How wrong this move is." I was a little agitated because we had planned to have everything loaded and leave by 1:00 pm. Our time was being pushed back by an hour already.

We finally got to the U-Haul place, and they did have the truck. As the lady was putting the order through, she said, "I've never seen this before. Hold on, I have to make a call." My mom's anxiety kicked in and she be-gan rubbing her hands through her hair and blowing hot air from her mouth.

I said, "Calm down. Dang, this is the last day you'll see me for a long time. Can we please make it halfway positive?"

She replied, "I'm going to the car. You can sit here and do this if you want to, but I'm not standing here waiting! This stuff [in nicer terms] is getting ridiculous!" Out the door she went, stomping.

Shaking my head, I turned around and the lady was talking to someone in the company. They explained to her that a previous U-Haul I had rented was not turned in on time and there was a balance to be paid. I refused to pay it, when I did turn it in but it was a day they were closed and they didn't check the truck in on time obviously. The church was purchasing the U-Haul on their account and I was not asking to pay the extra charge, when it was on the return store's behalf.

At the time, the only money I had was exactly enough to cover the gas expenses to get there and food to eat on the way. The lady across the counter handed me the phone and said, "Talk to them and see if it can be waived." She was not allowed to rent me the truck until this was taken care of.

In the meantime, my mom had walked back in, rushing me to come on! "Hurry up, I got things to do and I have to go to work," she said. Blocking her out, I continued to resolve my issue with the truck.

God's favor arose and they agreed to waive the fee. I handed the phone back to the lady and she finished up the details. I stood there anxious. What should have been done by 10:30 had now run into noon. Two hours to take care of getting this moving truck. I still had 35 minutes to get back to the house and begin loading it. My husband and girls were waiting on me to get there and had no clue as to what the wait was.

Finally, everything was back on track. We go out to check the truck and she explained, "This was a three-seat-er truck." My face lit up because I knew we could fit in it. The middle seat was big enough to buckle in both girls and the dog could sit in the floorboard area. It wasn't the safest method but it was the only one. Surprisingly, I felt like everything was going to be all right and not to worry.

Mom followed me back to the house. It was already a little after noon, so we were definitely not going to make time. We wanted to leave early because it was going to take nine hours or longer to get there in a U-Haul. We didn't want to be driving after dark very long, but we had to do what it took. Quickly, we loaded the truck and said our goodbyes to everyone. Our journey began and our new life awaited.

The long ride on the highway had just gotten started. A severe storm came through Kentucky. We were driving in treacherous conditions. As visibility was very limited and the strikes of lightning were strong, we continued driving cautiously. We drove in the storm for about 30 minutes and it passed over. When we got through it, the skies began clearing and the sun poked out.

A revelation came to me as I became thankful for the storm passing. God said, "Now you come out of the storms of life and peace is given to you." My heart fluttered and chill bumps overcame my limbs. I began realizing the storm does not determine where the ship goes. It's the captain who determines the direction. I was driving out of the valley of storms and into the light of prosperity.

From Kentucky we traveled through Ohio and then to Pure Michigan. As we crossed the state line, darkness of night had already begun setting in. The trip was over-all smooth and comfortable. We made our last stop to gas up before arriving at our new place. We had only enough for the gas and breakfast for the girls the next morning. So we got them donuts and milk, along with our gas. We were almost home.

We pulled up to our little yellow house with a brown garage door. A beautiful oak tree, stood tall in our front yard. We had not seen any pictures of the outside of the house, showing the details anyway. The inside we already knew we loved. We stepped out and stretched, excited to go in. We waited on a church member named Diamond to arrive with our keys. Diamond pulled in and brought us in for a tour. She lived here previously and had it all ready for us.

We couldn't believe this was really happening! It was like we had known her all of our lives. Joy and peace were taking place already. We talked a while and she left. It was after midnight, so we decided to leave everything on the truck and unpack in the morning. We would sleep on a sofa and love seat that were in the house. We got the girls comfortable, and we all fell fast asleep.

Early that morning, we woke up, ready to get settled in. Shaun and I didn't know how we were going to get the basic needs for the house and food to last us. I didn't allow it to dwell on my mind and discourage me. Shaun kept saying, "God's got us. We're going to be OK." We unloaded the truck and started putting things in their place. The girls loved their new rooms, and we made their area our main focus.

The phone rang, and on the other line was the secretary of the church. She began telling us how happy she was that we were here and she couldn't wait to see us. Then she said, "Pastor and his family are out of town. He told me to take care of anything you all need." We didn't want to tell her that we needed food, but my husband put pride to the side and explained our situation. She said, "Give me a few minutes and I'll come to pick your wife up to go shopping." God was already moving!!

She picked me up and we went to the local Meijer's. She told me, "Get everything you all need to last you." I felt so relieved and blessed that these people didn't even know us yet wanted to help us. That is something that's unheard of in this world today. Who would have imagined that all of this would happen so fast? Everything we needed was supplied. The vehicle issue was the only barrier we had left.

We got everything we needed, and I went home to put things away. I told my husband, "I want to take a walk and look for a job."

He gave me an "are you serious?" look. "We just got here, Babe" he said.

I chuckled and replied, "I would rather look now and have a better chance to get one sooner than wait until later." He already had a job promised, other than the church position he was in. So we knew income was going to come in, but I wanted to help out with the financial contribution, too.

We walked up and down the strip near our house. We enjoyed the breath of fresh air and difference in scenery. You could see the wide-open skies; back home the mountains blocked the sky level off. It was amazing to be in a new place where we had never lived before. While we walked I stopped and got applications at different places. We knocked out "two birds with one stone," as the old saying goes.

We got home, and I applied for different jobs on indeed. I was confident I would get a call back soon. So now I could put that burden at rest. We moved in on a Monday and that gave us time through the week to unpack and get the important stuff done before beginning our busy schedules. The church that we were brought to Michigan to commit to was vision oriented. There was structure in the business aspect, and we were required to attend weekly meetings. The leaders hit the ground running, and we did the same.

The church had two locations, a satellite ministry to reach out, Real Kids Paradise for the youth, dance ministry, drama ministry, and much more. This was something on a completely different level than what we were used to. They had dreams, vision, and unity. At the time, we questioned what we could bring to the table. We had little vision and counterfeit purposes all of our life, until now. The best thing we could offer was commitment, sacrifice, and the love for God that we had. That ended up being all we needed.

CHAPTER 20

Guilt, Hurt, Shame, But Not Defeat

We looked forward to our first Sunday of attending services with our new church family. We knew no one, had no family around, and we didn't know what to expect. Our one visit and phone conversations were all the time we had to get to know people. From those encounters, we already felt that we had a second family. It was so strange how we knew nothing about each other and still felt like we'd been around for a lifetime.

The first Sunday came. I was up hours before service started. I was so excited I couldn't sleep and started breakfast, then got ready. The girls were up and ready with no problem that morning, which was a surprise because usually I'd be dragging them out of bed. The nice lady, Alison, who was the secretary picked us up bright and early.

The church turned out to be less than five minutes from our house. We pulled up and my husband started his sound checks and getting prepared before service began. I hung out with the kids upstairs and waited to meet the children's ministry leaders. We took a peek at the kids' classes and we were amazed at how it was set up. It had very colorful paintings, lights, a mini stage, music, and more. It couldn't have been more perfect.

People started rolling in, and we got the kids signed in and situated. Shaun and I stood by the door to meet and shake hands. The love and genuine hearts of the people touched us in a special way. You could feel the presence of God in the atmosphere and that was the best feeling ever.

Shortly after, I found a seat toward the front and my husband sat to the side on his keyboard. I looked around me and just smiled. We really did it! God brought us here for a reason. I didn't know what it was, but I knew it was something special. I thought about the past few months of everything that took place, and I thought about what the future could bring. In that moment, I was just soaking up the happiness I felt.

The service began and everyone worshiped so freely. My husband did an amazing job on the music and with the praise team. His special gift is truly a blessing. I've been with him for years and still get a lot from his worship. I was so proud of him and the new steps he was taking in his ministry. He has worked so hard and sacrificed a lot over the years for music. I was so happy that these people saw the same thing I have always seen in him.

The pastor came up to begin preaching. Before delivering his message, he explained that the church was in the series of "Finding your purpose." He began his sermon, and I immediately felt conviction. I cried the entire time and couldn't help it. I knew God was at work. That's when an altar call took place.

He wasn't like most pastors we knew down south. He didn't call people out, beg them to come up, or show any type of force. He allowed God to move in the individuals and let them make the choice to receive it for themselves. I was one of the people who chose to get prayer.

In the pastor's sermon he talked about, "Finding your purpose, and how." He talked about "the difference in Purpose that God has for your life and counterfeit purpose, that we a lot of times find ourselves in." There was a lot of great views he pointed out: "What inspires you? Look at the people you're drawn to, what aggravates you the most, and what is your testimony?" A lot of times, our purpose lies within our testimony. As he preached this message, I gained vision of my purpose. I never imagined it being what God showed me it was.

After my emotional prayers that I left at the altar, I felt renewed and strengthened. I had all kinds of ideas and wrote them down as they came to mind. For once in my life, I felt like I could hold my head high. I was somebody!!! Maybe not much to the people who know me, but to God I was! In that moment, I started believing in myself. I went headfirst into my purpose and studied what I needed to pursue it.

After that service, a man walked up to us and gave us the keys to a well-kept Jeep SUV. He said, "It's yours to drive!" We cried, we jumped, and we lifted our hands! God just kept on blessing! The same week, my husband and I both had jobs, a vehicle, a home, and a new life. Yes, in one week all of this happened. We had found our purposes and were walking in them. When praises go up, blessings and favor rain down.

So I'm sure by now you're wondering what my purpose was. My testimony has everything to do with it. My purpose starts with being an advocate for victims of sexual assault and domestic violence. I pursued classes and started out as a volunteer. However, it goes far beyond that. There is more! I was told, "Dream Big! If your dream only takes you to achieve it, then you're not dreaming big enough."

I can say I am thankful for all the years of suffering. Due to the severity of my past, I can use what I've experienced to help others. To show people "that You can make it!" With God, I will help restore hope in the empty and not judge the weary. I stand in the gap of silence. I stand in the gap of hurt. I stand in the gap of pain, and I stand in the gap of fear! Finding my divine purpose has brought me to finding myself! It has not been easy, for the healing process is far worse than my experiences in the moment. I am free; I am alive. I have peace. I have joy, and I have strength! I'm no longer a victim, I am a Survivor!!

CHAPTER 21

My Old Kentucky Home

My life had changed under the ministry in Michigan. Our pastor took a new position in Georgia, and we followed him there. We knew God had connected us to his ministry, and we wanted to continue pursuing our destiny. However, we did move too fast, and he did not call us there for that specific time. Life in Georgia was much different and very expensive. We found ourselves struggling to rent after we were scammed upon our arrival. However, we did find a place and couldn't afford it.

The new church was about an hour from where we lived, and it was hard to commute. We were doing our best to survive. I know now that we were meant to go through that process because God was going to bring us out eventually. It was very hard though, and we decided that we were going to do whatever it took to survive. We allowed comfort to hold us captive, and made the choice to join another church temporarily.

We went shopping at a local Goodwill, and this pastor from another church was in line behind me at checkout. My husband had already taken our girls to the car. He turned around asked me who my husband was and what was his name. It sparked conversation, and he asked me to wait outside until he was finished because he needed to speak with him. I went to the car, and told my husband about this pastor. He said, "Babe, I'm ready to go. I'm not trying to wait." I insisted that I felt led to wait, and so we did.

This pastor came to the car, greeted him, and said, "God spoke to me and told me to bless you." He took money out of his wallet and handed it to my husband. Then, he reached down into his pocket and handed him more. We knew that God was working through him. We were almost completely broke and had very little. Soon after, we began going to that man's church because it was closer than our original church.

The church was a Southern Baptist style and a lot different from what we were used to. However, it was so full of love and acceptance. My husband became their worship leader, and they were like a second family to us. We found a house to rent through someone in the church and finally felt a little more settled. I say this because even when we moved too fast, and God knew that we were not ready for Georgia, he still kept us. His blessings still continued and never ceased. We were there for a little over a year and felt called back to Kentucky.

My husband had received a call from a former pastor he knew and was offered a position in Lexington, Kentucky. I did not ever want to go back to Kentucky because my life had completely changed from leaving there. I did not want to go back and face all of the shame I left behind, but it was meant to be. God was sending us back, and he did so quickly. We found an apartment in Lexington, loaded up the U-haul, and moved. My kids were transferred to so many different schools that I was nervous for them to have to transition again. However, they did very well because they were so young.

Upon moving back to Lexington and joining the new church, we were doing great. I found a wonderful job, and we were living so much more comfortably. Church was always so good, and we became close to the assistant pastor and his wife. My husband and I never had friends with whom we were really close like them. We were connected, took vacations together, and enjoyed ministry together.

God gave us a vision for a church where people could come and freely worship. He gave a vision to help the people that other churches didn't want. A year later, that vision came with provision, and it manifested. The church is more than we could have ever imagined. My husband is the worship leader, and I gave birth to my first women's ministry. On this journey, we have been blessed beyond understanding and are still very connected with our previous pastors. There is so much that God is doing, and destiny still awaits.

We have grown substantially in all aspects of life, and God has been doing a miraculous work. We have realized that all of this was a part of the process, and he took me back to my uncomfortable place for closure. He took me back to see if I would stand in the muddy waters. He took me back to finish the purifying process and heal the areas of my life that I tried to bury. Before coming back, I thought I was already healed, and I wasn't. I was from some things, but there were others that I had just buried.

Many blessings came from this journey. I grew a desire to proceed with getting my master's in social work. I have grown in every aspect of life. I have been able to be with my grandmother. My mom and I have a better relationship. My husband and I purchased our first home. Our girls are thriving in their schools, and we really feel loved by the people who surround us. I am truly thankful for all that God has done in our lives and is continuing to do. Every day I wake up, and I am thankful for life. I am grateful for the prayers that he did not answer, and I am thankful for the freedom in my spirit.

Sometimes things that happen in life make no sense and may leave us doubting God. If you will just hold on, he will see you through! Something has to break! You are not defined by the things you have done or what you have been through. Can I speak over your life for a moment? You are more than enough! The weapon may form but it won't prosper, and the enemy has no authority over you! I was the trash that God recycled. I was the statistic that should not have made it, and I did not have the education, knowledge, confidence, or strength to do anything with my life! I can give you an easy answer as to how it all happened—JESUS! When I fully surrendered, he did the rest.

The process of purification and healing took a long time. I wouldn't have shortened it now if I could. It was painful. It was uncomfortable, but it was rewarding. Many people turned their backs on me, but I learned that those people were not meant to go with me. What God has for us is for us. We cannot stop believing, and we must push until something happens. If I had given up, I would have died.

We are all created for a purpose, and it is important that we find out what that purpose is. I truly believe that we are put on earth to do what only God has for us to do. We get caught up in all that is happening and forget to seek him through it. It was in my place of darkness and desperation that I found him. Sure, he can blink his eye and take it all away, but why would you want that? Don't let the prophets prophesy you out of your dark place because it is in that place that you are being refined.

Lastly, if you can relate to the things that I have shared, I am here to say, "You will get through this." Please seek help if you need it. The time is now. The resources are out there, and please find someone you can trust to talk to. It is good to vent, let it out, and don't hold back. I don't care where you came from or where you have been, you are important! You can achieve anything that you want, if you truly want it. Invest in yourself because you are your greatest asset. If I have inspired you, my job here is done, and I pray that everyone who is reading this is blessed beyond their expectations.

TABATHA WILSON

INFORMATIONAL SOURCES ON DOMESTIC VIOLENCE AND SEXUAL ABUSE

Bennice, J. A., & Resick, P. A. (2003). Marital rape: History, research, and practice. *Trauma, Violence, & Abuse*, 4(3), 228–246.

Bergen, R. K. (1996). *Wife rape: Understanding the response of survivors and service provider*. Thousand Oaks, CA: Sage.

Bergen, R. K., & Barnhill, E. (2006, February). Marital rape: New research and directions. Retrieved from http://www.vawnet.org/applied-research-papers/print-"research-papers/print-document.php?doc_id=248

Black, M. C., Basile, K. C., Breiding, M. J., Smith, S. G., Walters, M. L., Merrick, M. T., Chen, J., & Stevens, M. R. (2011). *The national intimate partner and sexual violence survey (NISVS): 2010 summary report*. Atlanta, GA: National Center for Injury Prevention and Control, Centers for Disease Control and Prevention. Retrieved from http://www.cdc.gov/violenceprevention/pdf/nisvs_report2010-a.pdf

Breiding, M. J., & Amour, B. S. (2015). The association between disability and intimate partner violence in the United States. *Annals of Epidemiology*, 25(6), 455–457.

DeKeseredy, W., Rogness, M., & Schwartz, M. (2004). Separation/divorce sexual assault: The current state of social scientific knowledge. *Aggression and Violent Behavior*, 9, 675–691.

Kelly, T., & Stermac, L. Intimate partner sexual assault against women: Examining the impact and recommendations for clinical practice. *Partner Abuse*, 3(1), 107–122.

Jasinski, J., & Williams, L. (Eds.). (1998). Partner violence: *A Comprehensive review of 20 years of research*. Thousand Oaks, CA: Sage.

McFarlane, J., & Malecha, A. (2005). *Sexual assault among intimates: Frequency, consequences and treatments*. Retrieved from https://www.ojp.gov/pdffiles1/nij/grants/211678.pdf

NCADV. (2015, April 4). Quick guide: Domestic violence and sexual abuse. Retrieved from https://www.ncadv.org/blog/posts/quick-guide-domestic-violence-and-sexual-abuse

Rennison, C. M. (2002, August). Rape and sexual assault: Reporting to police and medical attention, 1992–2000. *Bureau of Justice Statistics: Selected Findings*, 1–4. Retrieved from https://bjs.ojp.gov/content/pub/pdf/rsarp00.pdf

Russell, D. E. H. (1990). *Rape in marriage*. New York: MacMillan.

Tjaden, P., & Thoennes, N. (2000, July). *Extent, nature, and consequences of intimate partner violence: Findings from the national violence against women survey*. Washington, DC: National Institute of Justice. Retrieved from https://www.ncjrs.gov/pdffiles1/nij/181867.pdf

The Apartment that my baby brother passed away in.
This is where it all began. As I went to take photos, I sat
in this parking lot and reflected on his memories. There
were few, but the ones that I did have are unforgettable.

The Apartments my granny lived in, and I moved to shortly after my brothers passing. This was a rough area.

The painful place where I lived at 9 years old. The place where my innocence was taken, and the place that it all began.

The Park where I would allow boys to touch me. It has cleaned up a lot since I was younger but still carries the same eerie feeling.

The exact apartment where all my troubles began. The drugs, alcohol, overdose, sex, secrets, manipulation, identity crisis, and more. It all happened within those four walls.

One of the hangout spots at the apartments.

The laundry room where sexual assault took place.

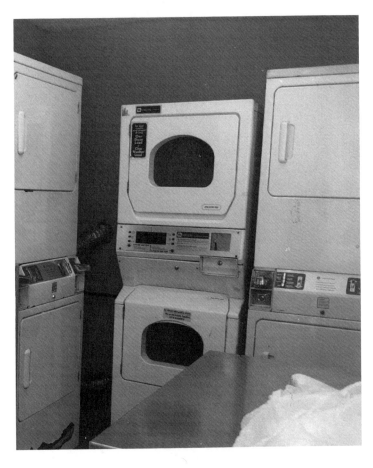

It was on that silver metal folding table that he sat and tried to force me to do sexual favors.

Reports obtained from the Rehab Treatment Center.
At first it was hard to see these, but now I realize that
I have come a long way. God was with me then and is
with me now.